First World War
and Army of Occupation
War Diary
France, Belgium and Germany

47 DIVISION
141 Infantry Brigade
London Regiment
17th (County of London) Battalion
(Poplar and Stepney Rifles)
9 March 1915 - 16 October 1916

WO95/2737/1

The Naval & Military Press Ltd
www.nmarchive.com
Published in association with The National Archives

Published by

The Naval & Military Press Ltd

Unit 10 Ridgewood Industrial Park,

Uckfield, East Sussex,

TN22 5QE England

Tel: +44 (0) 1825 749494

www.naval-military-press.com

www.nmarchive.com

This diary has been reprinted in facsimile from the original. Any imperfections are inevitably reproduced and the quality may fall short of modern type and cartographic standards.

© Crown Copyright
Images reproduced by permission of The National Archives, London, England, 2015.

Contents

Document type	Place/Title	Date From	Date To
Heading	War Diary 1/17th Battalion London Regiment From 9th March 1915 To 13th October 1916		
Heading	1/17th Battalion London Regt From March 9th 1915 To June 30th 1916		
War Diary	St Albans-Southampton	09/03/1915	09/03/1915
War Diary	Havre	10/03/1915	11/03/1915
War Diary	Havre-Cassel	11/03/1915	11/03/1915
War Diary	Cassel	12/03/1915	12/03/1915
War Diary	Winnezeele	18/03/1915	18/03/1915
War Diary	St Venant	19/03/1915	19/03/1915
War Diary	Hurionville	22/03/1915	22/03/1915
War Diary	Hurionville	27/03/1915	27/03/1915
War Diary	Hurionville	07/04/1915	07/04/1915
War Diary	Bethune	08/04/1915	19/04/1915
War Diary	Le Plantin	20/04/1915	23/04/1915
War Diary	Gorre	24/04/1915	25/04/1915
War Diary	Gorre and Le Plantin	26/04/1915	26/04/1915
War Diary	Le Plantin	27/04/1915	27/04/1915
War Diary	Le Plantin and Gorre	28/04/1915	28/04/1915
War Diary	Gorre	29/04/1915	29/04/1915
War Diary	Gorre and Le Plantin	30/04/1915	30/04/1915
War Diary	Le Plantin	01/05/1915	03/05/1915
War Diary	Le Plantin and Gorre	04/05/1915	04/05/1915
War Diary	Gorre & La Beuvriere	05/05/1915	05/05/1915
War Diary	La Beuvriere	06/05/1915	07/05/1915
War Diary	La Beuvriere Tessars	08/05/1915	08/05/1915
War Diary	Essars & La Touret	09/05/1915	09/05/1915
War Diary	La Touret And La Couture	10/05/1915	10/05/1915
War Diary	La Couture & Le Falon	11/05/1915	11/05/1915
War Diary	Le Falon & Beuvry	12/05/1915	12/05/1915
War Diary	Givenchy (Pont Fixe)	13/05/1915	31/05/1915
War Diary	Givenchy (Pont Fixe) & Bethune	01/06/1915	01/06/1915
War Diary	Bethune & Cambrain	02/06/1915	02/06/1915
War Diary	Trafford Hall	09/03/1915	09/03/1915
War Diary	Havre	10/03/1915	10/03/1915
War Diary	Hurionville	22/03/1915	22/03/1915
War Diary	Festubert Trenches	08/04/1915	14/04/1915
War Diary	Le Plantin	19/04/1915	23/04/1915
War Diary	Gorre	24/04/1915	24/04/1915
War Diary	Le Plantin	27/04/1915	04/05/1915
War Diary	Gorre	04/05/1915	04/05/1915
War Diary	La Beuvriere	05/05/1915	05/05/1915
War Diary	Essars	08/05/1915	09/05/1915
War Diary	La Touret	09/05/1915	09/05/1915
War Diary	La Couture	10/05/1915	10/05/1915
War Diary	Lacon	11/05/1915	11/05/1915
War Diary	Beury	12/05/1915	12/05/1915
War Diary	Givenchy	13/05/1915	13/05/1915
War Diary	Givenchy (Pont Fixe)	14/05/1915	22/05/1915
War Diary	Givenchy	23/05/1915	01/06/1915

War Diary	Bethune	01/06/1915	02/06/1915
War Diary	Cambrin	02/06/1915	04/06/1915
War Diary	Annequin	04/06/1915	05/06/1915
War Diary	Verquin	06/06/1915	07/06/1915
War Diary	Le Phillosophe	07/06/1915	09/06/1915
War Diary	Fosse No7	09/06/1915	11/06/1915
War Diary	Cambrin	03/06/1915	04/06/1915
War Diary	Cambrin and Annequin	04/06/1915	04/06/1915
War Diary	Annequin	05/06/1915	05/06/1915
War Diary	Annequin & Verquin	06/06/1915	06/06/1915
War Diary	Verquin and Le Phillosophe	07/06/1915	07/06/1915
War Diary	Le Philosophe	08/06/1915	08/06/1915
War Diary	Le Phillosophe And Fosse No7	09/06/1915	09/06/1915
War Diary	E. Of. Village Fosse No. 7	10/06/1915	12/06/1915
War Diary	La Philosophe & Mazingarbe	13/06/1915	16/06/1915
War Diary	La Philosophe & Mazingarbe	17/06/1915	17/06/1915
War Diary	Le Philosophe	16/06/1915	16/06/1915
War Diary	E Of Village. Fosse. No 7 Le Philosophe Mazingarbe & Noeux-Les Mines.	17/06/1915	17/06/1915
War Diary	Noeux-Les Mines.	18/06/1915	19/06/1915
War Diary	Noeux-Les Mines And Les Brebis	20/06/1915	20/06/1915
War Diary	Les Brebis	21/06/1915	23/06/1915
War Diary	Les Brebis & Bully Grenay	24/06/1915	24/06/1915
War Diary	Bully Grenay	25/06/1915	02/07/1915
War Diary	South Maroc	03/07/1915	06/07/1915
War Diary	Mazingarbe	07/07/1915	13/07/1915
War Diary	Mazingarbe And E. Of Village Fosse No. 7 S Of Le Philosophe	14/07/1915	14/07/1915
War Diary	E. Of Village Fosse No. 7 S Of Le Philosophe (X.2. Section)	15/07/1915	16/07/1915
War Diary	E. Of Village Fosse No. 7 South Of Le Philosophe (X Section Sub Sector X. 2)	17/07/1915	18/07/1915
War Diary	Le Philosophe	19/07/1915	22/07/1915
War Diary	Le Philosophe & Fosse No. 7	23/07/1915	23/07/1915
War Diary	Fosse No. 7 X Section Sub Sector X.2	24/07/1915	26/07/1915
War Diary	Fosse No. 7 X Section Sub Sector X.2 and Le Philosophe	27/07/1915	27/07/1915
War Diary	Le Philosophe	28/07/1915	29/07/1915
War Diary	Le Philosophe and South Maroc	30/07/1915	30/07/1915
War Diary	South Maroc W. Section	31/07/1915	31/07/1915
War Diary	Noeux-Les-Mines	02/08/1915	02/08/1915
War Diary	Noeux-Les-Mines and Allouagne	03/08/1915	03/08/1915
War Diary	Allougne	04/08/1915	15/08/1915
War Diary	Allouagne and Houchin	18/08/1915	18/08/1915
War Diary	Houchin (in Bivouacs In Wood) and Les Brebis	19/08/1915	25/08/1915
War Diary	Les Brebis	25/08/1915	30/08/1915
War Diary	Houchin	31/08/1915	03/09/1915
War Diary	Houchin and Les-brebis	04/09/1915	04/09/1915
War Diary	Les-Brebis	05/09/1915	05/09/1915
War Diary	Les Brebis and Noeux Les-Mines	06/09/1915	12/09/1915
War Diary	Les Brebis	13/09/1915	14/09/1915
War Diary	Houchin	16/09/1915	20/09/1915
War Diary	Les Brebis	21/09/1915	24/09/1915
War Diary	N. Maroc	25/09/1915	01/10/1915
War Diary	Vaudricourt	02/10/1915	03/10/1915
War Diary	Hesdigneul	03/10/1915	06/10/1915

War Diary	Houchin	06/10/1915	12/10/1915
War Diary	Mazingarbe	12/10/1915	14/10/1915
War Diary	Loos	14/10/1915	29/10/1915
War Diary	Loos	30/10/1915	30/10/1915
War Diary	Le Philosophe	31/10/1915	05/11/1915
War Diary	Old German Second Line Trench In Local Reserve	06/11/1915	06/11/1915
War Diary	Loos (frond Line) B Section In Reserve In Old German 2nd Line	07/11/1915	07/11/1915
War Diary	Loose (front line) B Sector in reserve in Oed German 2nd Line	08/11/1915	10/11/1915
War Diary	Loose (B Sector) Front Line	11/11/1915	12/11/1915
War Diary	Loose (B Sector) Front Line and Le Philosophe	13/11/1915	13/11/1915
War Diary	Le Philosophe and Lille RS.	13/11/1915	13/11/1915
War Diary	Lillers and Burbure	15/11/1915	15/11/1915
War Diary	Burbure	16/11/1915	01/12/1915
War Diary	On & Trek	02/12/1915	02/12/1915
War Diary	Burbure	03/12/1915	12/12/1915
War Diary	Burbure & Sailly Labourse	13/12/1915	14/12/1915
War Diary	Vermelles	15/12/1915	16/12/1915
War Diary	Noyelles	17/12/1915	18/12/1915
War Diary	Vaudricourt	20/12/1915	22/12/1915
War Diary	Sailly Labourse and in D Sector	23/12/1915	24/12/1915
War Diary	Sailly Labourse	30/12/1915	30/12/1915
War Diary	Verquin	31/12/1915	02/01/1916
War Diary	Verquin & Lebrebis	03/01/1916	04/01/1916
War Diary	Les brebis & Loos	04/01/1916	04/01/1916
War Diary	Loos N. Sub Sector	05/01/1916	07/01/1916
War Diary	N. Maroc	07/01/1916	07/01/1916
War Diary	Loos	08/01/1916	08/01/1916
War Diary	Loos N Sub Sector	09/01/1916	12/01/1916
War Diary	Les Brebis	13/01/1916	15/01/1916
War Diary	Les Brebis & S. Maroc	16/01/1916	16/01/1916
War Diary	Maroc	17/01/1916	17/01/1916
War Diary	Maroc Sector Right Subsector	18/01/1916	22/01/1916
War Diary	Maroc Right Subsector	23/01/1916	23/01/1916
War Diary	Maroc Bracquemont.	24/01/1916	24/01/1916
War Diary	Maroc & Bracquemont	24/01/1916	24/01/1916
War Diary	Bracquemont	25/01/1916	27/01/1916
War Diary	Bracquemont & Loos	28/01/1916	28/01/1916
War Diary	Loos	29/01/1916	29/02/1916
War Diary	Loos	30/01/1916	04/02/1916
War Diary	Loos & Le Brebis	05/02/1916	05/02/1916
War Diary	Maroc	10/02/1916	14/02/1916
War Diary	Maroc & Les Brebis	15/02/1916	15/02/1916
War Diary	Burbure	17/02/1916	03/03/1916
War Diary	Burbure & Bomy	04/03/1916	04/03/1916
War Diary	Bomy	05/03/1916	08/03/1916
War Diary	Bomy & Sains Les Pernes	09/03/1916	09/03/1916
War Diary	Sains Les Pernes & Camblain Chatalain	10/03/1916	10/03/1916
War Diary	Chamblain Chatelain	11/03/1916	14/03/1916
War Diary	Camblain Chatelain & Villers Au Bois	15/03/1916	16/03/1916
War Diary	Villers Au Bois & Carency Sector	16/03/1916	16/03/1916
War Diary	Carency Sector & Villers Au Bois	20/03/1916	21/03/1916
War Diary	Villers Au Bois & Fresnicourt	21/03/1916	21/03/1916
War Diary	Fresnicourt	22/03/1916	26/03/1916
War Diary	Fresnicourt & Villers Au Bois	27/03/1916	01/04/1916

War Diary	Villers A-B	28/03/1916	31/04/1916
War Diary	Villers Au Bois & Carency Sector	01/04/1916	01/04/1916
War Diary	Carency Sector	02/04/1916	06/04/1916
War Diary	Carency Sector & Villers	07/04/1916	07/04/1916
War Diary	Villers & Fresnicourt	08/04/1916	14/04/1916
War Diary	Fresnicourt	09/04/1916	13/04/1916
War Diary	Fresnicourt & Villers	14/04/1916	14/04/1916
War Diary	Villers	15/04/1916	18/04/1916
War Diary	Carency Sector & Villers	19/04/1916	19/04/1916
War Diary	Carency Sector	20/04/1916	20/04/1916
War Diary	Carency	21/04/1916	24/04/1916
War Diary	Carency & Villers	25/04/1916	25/04/1916
War Diary	Villers & Fresnicourt	26/04/1916	26/05/1916
War Diary	Fresnicourt	27/04/1916	01/05/1916
War Diary	Fresnicourt & Villers	02/05/1916	02/05/1916
War Diary	Villers & Carency Sector	07/05/1916	07/05/1916
War Diary	Carency	08/05/1916	12/05/1916
War Diary	Carency & Villers	13/05/1916	13/05/1916
War Diary	Villers & Verdrel	14/05/1916	14/05/1916
War Diary	Verdrel	15/05/1916	18/05/1916
War Diary	Verdrel & Gouy Servins	19/05/1916	19/05/1916
War Diary	Gouy Servins-Villers	20/05/1916	20/05/1916
War Diary	Carency	21/05/1916	25/05/1916
War Diary	Maisnel Bouche & Dieval	26/05/1916	26/05/1916
War Diary	Dieval	27/05/1916	10/06/1916
War Diary	Dieval & Fosse 10	11/06/1916	12/06/1916
War Diary	Bully	13/06/1916	15/06/1916
War Diary	Bully & Fosse 10	17/06/1916	17/06/1916
War Diary	Fosse	18/06/1916	21/06/1916
War Diary	Angres L Subsector	22/06/1916	25/06/1916
War Diary	In Bde Reserve	26/06/1916	28/06/1916
War Diary	Support	29/06/1916	30/06/1916
Heading	War Diary From 1st August 1916 To 18-10-16	18/10/1916	18/10/1916
War Diary	Moncheaux & Bonniers	01/08/1916	01/08/1916
War Diary	Bonniers	01/08/1916	03/08/1916
War Diary	Maison Ponthieu	04/08/1916	04/08/1916
War Diary	Maison Ponthieu & Argenvillers	05/08/1916	05/08/1916
War Diary	Argenvillers	06/08/1916	19/08/1916
War Diary	Bruchamp	20/08/1916	20/08/1916
War Diary	Monton Villers	21/08/1916	21/08/1916
War Diary	Pierregot	22/08/1916	22/08/1916
War Diary	Bresle	23/08/1916	10/09/1916
War Diary	Support	11/09/1916	11/09/1916
War Diary	Mametz Wood	12/09/1916	13/09/1916
War Diary	High Wood	14/09/1916	16/09/1916
War Diary	Mametz Wood	17/09/1916	17/09/1916
War Diary	Switch Line	18/09/1916	19/09/1916
War Diary	Albert	20/09/1916	20/09/1916
War Diary	Bresle	21/09/1916	26/09/1916
War Diary	Bresle & Mametz	27/09/1916	27/09/1916
War Diary	Trenches Before Eaucourt L'abbe	29/09/1916	01/10/1916
War Diary	In Line	02/10/1916	05/10/1916
War Diary	Mametz Wood	06/10/1916	08/10/1916
War Diary	Mile Street	09/10/1916	10/10/1916
War Diary	Framvillers	11/10/1916	14/10/1916
War Diary	Bussus Bussus	15/10/1916	16/10/1916

War Diary

Army Confidential

1/17th Battalion London Regiment
— Poplar and Stepney Rifles —

From 9th March 1915
to
5th October 1916

1/17th Battalion London Regt.

From March. 9th 1915
To June 30. 1916

17th BATTN. LONDON REGT.
(POPLAR–STEPNEY RIFLES)

Tuesday March 9th 1915 - ST ALBANS - SOUTHAMPTON
Battalion left St Albans for Southampton, and embarked on S/S "VIPER" and "TRAFFORD HALL"

Wednesday March 10th 1915 @ HAVRE.
Battalion disembarked at HAVRE at 9am and marched to No 1 Rest Camp ST ADRESSE.

Thursday March 11th 1915 @ HAVRE – CASSEL
Battalion left Rest Camp at 10am and entrained Havre on via AMIENS — ST OMER to CASSEL

Friday March 12th 1915 @ CASSEL
Detrained at CASSEL and marched to billets at WINNEZEELE.

MARCH 13TH, 14TH, 15TH, 16TH AND 17TH @ WINNEZEELE

Thursday March 18th 1915 @ WINNEZEELE
Battalion left WINNEZEELE at 6am and marched to a rendezvous W of STEENVOORDE, entrained on 42 Motor buses, thence via HAZEBROUCK to a point 3 miles S.N. the Battalion then proceeded by march route to ST VENANT, where we halted into billets.
The transport horses had marched the previous night to the same place

Friday March 19th 1915 @ ST VENANT AND HURIONVILLE.
Battn: left ST VENANT and marched to LILLERS – LE REVEILON – ALLOUAGNE to HURIONVILLE and billeted

MARCH 20TH AND 21ST @ HURIONVILLE

Monday March 22nd 1915 @ HURIONVILLE
Battn inspected @ 2p.m., drawn up in Column of route, by Field Marshal Sir John French and Maj- General Munro.

March 22ND, 23RD, 24TH, 25TH AND 26TH @ HURIONVILLE

Saturday March 27th 1915 @ HURIONVILLE
Parties of 4 officers and 4 N.C.O's proceeded to RICHEBURG L ST VAAST daily to spend 24 hours in the Trenches opposite the BOIS DUBIEZ attached to the 2nd WELSH REGIMENT for instruction.

From March 29TH to April 6TH Battalion billeted at HURIONVILLE.

Wednesday April 7th 1915 @ HURIONVILLE AND BETHUNE.
Battalion left HURIONVILLE @ 11am and marched via ALLOUAGNE — CHOQUES to billets in MONTMORENCY BARRACKS at BETHUNE.

Thursday April 8th 1915 @ BETHUNE.
At 6pm. A. Coy marched to FESTUBERT trenches attached to WORCESTER REGIMENT for 24 hours { NO CASUALTIES
Same time B. Coy marched to FESTUBERT trenches attached to GLASGOW HIGHLANDERS { ONE CASUALTY No 1644 Pte Antonovitch slightly wounded shot thro' muscle of right arm

Friday April 9th 1915 @ BETHUNE

At 6pm C. Coy marched to FESTUBERT trenches attached to WORCESTER REGT. for 24 hours. 2 Casualties Pte Gilmour J & Pte Wellington D (Shell wounds in face) (Shell wounds in calf)

D Coy supplied working parties of 200 men in two relief 100 men 60 Shovels. No Casualties.

Saturday April 10th 1915 @ BETHUNE

At 6pm D. Coy marched to FESTUBERT trenches attached to WORCESTER REGT. for 24 hours. No Casualties.

B. Coy supplied working parties of 200 men in two reliefs 100 men 60 Shovels. No Casualties

Sunday April 11th 1915 @ BETHUNE

At 6pm A. Coy marched to FESTUBERT trenches attached to WORCESTER REGT for 24 hours. No Casualties

C. Coy supplied working party 200 men in two reliefs 100 men 60 Shovels. No Casualties

Monday April 12th 1915 @ BETHUNE

At 6pm B. Coy marched to FESTUBERT trenches attached to WORCESTER REGT for 24 hours. No Casualties

A Coy supplied working party 200 men in two reliefs 100 men 60 Shovels. No Casualties

Tuesday April 13th 1915 @ BETHUNE

At 6pm C. Coy marched to FESTUBERT trenches attached to WORCESTER REGT. for 24 hours. No Casualties.

A. Coy supplied working party 200 men in two reliefs 100 men 60 Shovels. No Casualties

Wednesday April 14th 1915 @ BETHUNE

D. Coy @ 6pm marched to FESTUBERT trenches attached to WORCESTER REGT. for 24 hours 2 Casualties (Gunshot wounds in hand) Pte Sankey A. 9907 (Contused wound) (16147) S. Blackburn (Richard)

Pte Rockwood 3252. (Injury to throat (Strangulated)

B. Coy supplied working parties of 200 men in two reliefs 100 men 60 shovels. No Casualties.

Thursday April 15th @ BETHUNE

Work in trenches @ FESTUBERT finished

April 16th, 17th and 18th Battalion @ BETHUNE

Sunday April 18th 1915. @ BETHUNE

Commanding Officer and Adjutant visited 5th Brigade Office to receive Instructions re work for the following week.

Monday April 19th 1915 @ BETHUNE

Battalion ~~took~~ took over billets of Royal
Inniskilling Fusiliers @ LE PLANTIN, about two
miles N.E. of Bethune.
B. & D. Coys "Headquarters Staff" marched off
at 1-30 p.m. and took over different billets and
Headquarters of ROYAL INNISKILLING FUSILIERS.
A. & C. ~~Coys~~ detached off to MONT BERNENCHY BARROWS
not given
Rations took over trenches occupied by R. Inniskilling Fus.
Working parties supplied by B. and D. Coy's
1st Relief B Coy B'tns 2nd Relief D. Coy 6p.m. till 2a.m.
Reported aid post 30cbts R. of Batn. Headquarters
1 Casualty C. Coy 1 Casualty A. Coy (Slight wounds)
7652. Sgt. Smith C.A. {Slight wounds rejoined ~~not~~ Batn to change
14452. Rfn. Heal.G {Slight wound rejoined Batn LE PLANTIN
@ LE PLANTIN

Tuesday April 20th 1915 @ LE PLANTIN

No change of Coys in trenches
1st Relief B. Coy RFNS. 2nd Relief D. Coy RFNS.
8p.m. 12Mdnight.6.5ft. — do — 12Mdnight to 4a.m.
No Casualty.

Wednesday April 21st 1915 @ LE PLANTIN

B & D Coys relieved A & C Coys in the trenches
Working parties supplied by B. & D. Coys. A. Coy
left 2 Platoons in trenches @ time of relief of Coys &
consolidated fire trench party 8p.m. till 12midnight.
No Casualty. — do — 2midnight till 4am

Thursday April 22nd 1915 @ LE PLANTIN

No change of Coy's in trenches. One Casualty D. Coy
Working parties supplied by A. & C. Coys.
A Coy first working party 2 platoons 8p.m. till 12noon ??
C. Coy second — do — 12mdngt till 4a.m.

Friday April 23rd 1915 @ LE PLANTIN

No change of Coys in trenches.
Working party not supplied by our Regiment
One Casualty { Rfn. Kellman J.G. No 1613
 { Seriously wounded in action
Battalion moved to rest billets in GORRE A& D
Coys @ no R@no moved @ 4pm 16 B.D. Coys moved off
when relieved at trenches.

Saturday April 24th. 1915 @ GORRE.

Battalion left billets and took over billets occupied
by HIGHLAND LIGHT INFANTRY @ GORRE. @ 4pm.
B & D. Coys remained in their billets after previous night
No 1613 Rfn. Kellman J.G. died of wounds Buried BETHUNE Cathedral.

Sunday. April 25th. 1915 @ GORRE.

No change.

Monday April 26th 1915 @ GORRE and LE PLANTIN

Battalion relieved 19th Battalion in the first line @ LE PLANTIN. A & C. Coy. in trenches. Platoon No. 1 D. Coy. B & D. Coy. in Support billets in the trenches. Working parties supplied by B & D. Coy in two reliefs of 2 Platoons per Company. No Casualties.

Tuesday April 27th 1915 @ LE PLANTIN

No change in trenches or supports. Working parties supplied by B & D Companies without incident. One casualty A Coy. 2253 Pue. E. J. [?]

Wednesday April 28th 1915. @ LE PLANTIN and GORRE.

No change in trenches until 9 pm when Battalion relieved by 19th Battalion in the first line. B & D Coys H.Q.s left front line at 4 pm and arrived GORRE @ 5 pm. A & C Coys arrived @ GORRE @ 10 pm. No Casualties.

Thursday April 29th. 1915. @ GORRE.

Battalion in reserve. Nothing of importance happened.

Friday April 30th. 1915 @ GORRE. and LE PLANTIN

Battalion relieved 19th Battalion in first line @ LE PLANTIN. B & D Coys took over trenches @ 8 pm (also Platoon No 1 on night) A & C Coys took over Reserve billets redoubts @ 4 pm. No casualties supplied working parties of 2 platoons in 2 reliefs.

Saturday May 1st 1915 @ LE PLANTIN.

No change of Coys in trenches. No Casualties. A & C Coys supplies working parties 2 platoons per Coy in two reliefs. No Casualties.

Sunday May 2nd. @ LE PLANTIN.

B & D Coys relieved by A & C Coys in trenches @ 8 pm. B Coy. supplied working party. D Coy supplied party for wood & water fatigue.

Monday May 3rd. @ LE PLANTIN

No change in trenches. Two casualties early morn. by shell from our own artillery. Casualties 11290 Pte A. Stewart. wounded in thigh. 1st Pte A. Coy. 2454 Pte W. Shipp. J. wounded in shoulder. 1st A & B Coy working party. D Coy fatigue party for wood & water.

Tuesday May 4th. @ LE PLANTIN & GORRE

No change in trenches. Battalion relieved by 6th City of London Rifles in the first line. A & D relieved with B & D Coys (Rupfest) reserve billets respectively) at 4 pm. A & C Coys relieved in trenches @ 8 pm. Battn. took over Reserve Billets at TUNING FORK occupied by 6th C. L. Rifles. One Casualty. No 1855 Cpl. Johnson J. wounded early morning on YELLOW ROAD (Sniper or Stray Shot?)

Wednesday May 5th 1915 @ GORRE & LA BEUVRIERE
Battalion were relieved by 8th Battalion City of London Rifles in the Reserve billets @ GORRE at 2 pm. Batta. then marched to LA BEUVRIERE by Coys @ 15 minutes intervals. Batta. took over billets and reported all correct at 4.30 p.m.

Thursday May 6th 1915 @ LA BEUVRIERE
No change.

Friday May 7th 1915 @ LA BEUVRIERE
Battalion received orders to be ready to move at a minutes notice. Battalion ready but did not move off.

Saturday May 8th 1915 @ LA BEUVRIERE & ESSARS.
Battalion still in readiness for move. Battalion moved off with 1st line transport @ midnight and marched via CHOCQUES and BETHUNE to ESSARS. Arrived and took over billets about 4 am. 9/5/15 Battalion attached to 2nd Division under Major General Horne.

Sunday May 9th 1915 @ ESSARS & LA TOURET.
At 5 am Battalion in Joint Army Reserve during the attack on the enemies lines Battalion evacuated billets @ ESSARS and marched to LA TOURET at 9 pm. Everyone in billets & all correct at 11.50 p.m.

Monday May 10th 1915 @ LA TOURET and LA COUTURE
Battalion received orders to change billets and to be clear by 4 pm. Battalion took over new billets and H.Q. at LA COUTURE. Battalion still part of first Army Reserve.

Tuesday May 11th 1915 @ LA COUTURE & LE FALON
Battalion received orders to move H.Q. from S. J. LA COUTURE to E. J. LACON. Batt still in reserve. Battalion H.Q. evacuated @ 9 am and new ones directly taken over.

Wednesday May 12th 1915 @ LE FALON & BEUVRY.
Battalion received orders re change of billets. Left (4 pm) LACON and marched in column of route to BEUVRY. New designation of 2nd London Division to 4-4th (London) Division and 5th London Infantry Bde to 141st Infantry Brigade. Batter rejoined 47th (2nd London) Division.

Thursday May 13th 1915 @ BEUVRY and GIVENCHY (PONT FIXE)
Battalion went fr tents nr tracks by Lob to relieve
Camerons. Battalion received orders to move at once and
take over line vacated by the CAMERONS at GIVENCHY
A & C coys in trenches. B & D coys to supports.
No casualties.

Friday May 14th 1915 @ GIVENCHY (PONT FIXE)
No change of coys in trenches. Casualties two. B coy
No 2630. Rfn. Donington J. Killed in action and Buried :—
PONT FIXE. A.14. Ref. Map. BETHUNE 1/40,000. A coy.
No 3226. Rfn. Bought severely wounded.

Saturday May 15th 1915 @ GIVENCHY (PONT FIXE)
A & B coys in trenches until 6pm. B & D coys
relieves A & C coys in front line and relief
complete at 6pm. A & C coys fall back to
support. Two casualties. A coy. 2855 Rfn.
Cartney J. C coy. 2369. Rfn. Waldick E.

Sunday May 16th 1915 @ GIVENCHY (PONT FIXE)
B & D coys in trenches. Trench Mortar exploded
in trenches injuring top of Trench Mortar Battery.
Gunner was Shrapnel with effect. B men. Killed
and 4 wounded badly.

Monday May 17th 1915 @ GIVENCHY.
B & D coys in trenches. A & C coys in support.
No coy in Reserve.

Sunday May 16th 1915 @ GIVENCHY (PONT FIXE) (continued)
Casualties as follows. Trench Mortar Battery. No 1953
Cpl. Hardes P. Killed Wounded by Shrapnel.
near Distillery No 668 Rfn Burney J (Killed) A Coy.
No 2115. Rfn Savery E. (killed) A No 1891 Sgt Joden (C Coy)
in Bn. (Died of wounds) All three buried at PONT FIXE
GIVENCHY. A.14. Ref. Map. BETHUNE 1/40,000. In
a garden 30 yds s of the Post Office. Wounded by shrapnel.
No 1644/cpl Ritherige A.J. C Coy.: No 2041 Rfn.
Jenny W. A Coy. No 2567 Rfn Holloway. R.S.
C Coy. No 3202 Rfn Crickmore S. A Coy
Burial of Savery & Burney took place in the afternoon.

Monday May 17th 1915 @ GIVENCHY (PONT FIXE)
B & D Companies in the trenches. A Coy
in Support. C Coy in Reserve. Casualties
(3) No 2303 Rfn. Unwin L.S. Wounded by
Shrapnel (B Coy) 1445. Rfn. Fisher George
Bellebourne of Shrodies. (B Coy) 2343 Rfn
Carter. E (Killed) Shot through head.
Buried A.9. d.44. Ref. Map. BETHUNE 1/40,000.
Sgt Joden buried. Lt Walters officiated.
Adjutant had a narrow escape, shells hitting
Bridge House. PONT FIXE and PONT FIXE BRIDGE
while he was trickling hat gunfire.

Tuesday May. 18th. 1915. @ GIVENCHY (PONT FIXE)
B & D. Companies in trenches until 4pm.
Relief takes place. A & C. Companies going into trenches and B & D. Coys. take up support & reserve. D. Coy. support. B. Company Reserve. Distillery and around Pont Fixe shelled pretty heavily and shelled nearly all night. Casualty one. No. 2556. Rfm Adams. H. J. (B Coy) wounded by bullet in arm.

Wednesday May. 19th. 1915 @ GIVENCHY (PONT FIXE)
A & C. Coys in front line trenches. D. Coy in support. B. Coy in Reserve. Transport coming along Canal bank in close order was seen apparently by German Artillery Observation Post and the result was the shelling of the Distillery, Canal Bank, and Bridge at PONT FIXE. One shell fell just outside H.Q. wounding one man severely and another slight, also wounded 1 Mule. I severely having to be destroyed by Brigade Veterinary Officer. One shell bursting in distillery wounded two men and one falling into Bridge fence injuring another two Officers servants

Casualties:- (A Coy) No 2003. Leipaller I. A. Hughes. (wound of Skull Kemmiterini) (B Coy) 14/55 Rfn Younger. A. V. Shell wound of ear < chin. (facial paralysis) (A Coy) 2874 Rfm Aggis. A. Splints wound of Skull. (B Coy) 2981 Rfm Pavey. H. G. Shell wound of Thorax. (serious) (C Coy) 2031 Rfm Williamson R. Lw. wound of fore arm.

Thursday May. 20th. 1915 @ GIVENCHY (PONT FIXE)
A & C. Coys in front line up to 4pm. Relieved by B & D. Companies and relief completed by 6pm. A & C. Coys take up support & Reserve trenches respectively. Things very quiet all day. No Casualties.

Friday May. 21st. 1915 @ GIVENCHY (PONT FIXE)
B & D. Companies in front line. A. Coy support. C. Coy Reserves. Canadians on our left attacked after bombardment of the enemy by our Artillery reported to have taken line of trenches this Confirmed also reported that Germans made a counter attack against the Canadians. No Casualties.

Note:
Pont Fixe named at PONTFIXE is Bridge that crosses the canal at Distillery

Saturday. May. 22nd. @ GIVENCHY. (PONT FIXE)

B.D. Companies in trenches up to 4 p.m. relieved by A.C. Companies. B + D. Coys falling back to Support Reserve trenches respectively. Germans shelled Festubert, Bridge, and around Pont Fixé very heavily during the early hours of the morning. Draft of 1 Officer & 20. N.C.O's Men arrived from first reinforcement @ the Base. Draft included 2/Lieut. E.J. Carter, also Rfn. Hollington & Stokes Bean who was wounded at Festubert on April 14th 1915. 1914?. Everything fairly quiet. No Casualties.

Sunday (Whit-Sunday) May. 23rd @ GIVENCHY (PONT FIXE)

A. C. Coys in front line. B. Coy in supports. D. Coy in Reserve. Fighting still going on heavily on our left. Fictitious attack K.5. Casualties:– C. Coy. Cpl. Whitear. J. Killed in action, bet. Shrapnel. 6 bullets wounds of body. (Reg.No 1866) B. Coy. No. 2860. Rfn Strauss. L. Seriously injured. not expected to live.

(Whit-Monday. May. 24th. 1915 @ GIVENCHY (PONT FIXE)

Italy declare war on Austria from this date (officially confirmed). No. 2860. Rfn. Strauss L. C. coy reported as seriously wounded yesterday died of wounds. Burial of No.1866.Cpl. Whitear J. of C. Coy took place @ 11 am. Buried A.14. (PONT FIXE) GIVENCHY. W. of Post Office about 30 yds. Ref Map BETHUNE 1/40,000. A & D. Coys in front line trenches till 4 p.m. B + C. Coys in Supports Reserve trenches respectively till 4 p.m. A & D. Coys relieved by B & C. Companies in front line. C. and A. Coys fell back to Support Reserve trenches respectively.
Relief completed by 11 p.m. No further casualties.

Tuesday – May. 25th. 1915 @ GIVENCHY (PONT FIXE)

B. and D. Companies in trenches. No. 2860. Rfn Strauss L. C. Coy buried at 11 am. @ (PONT FIXE) GIVENCHY. A.14. 30 yds W. of Post Office in a Garden. Ref Map Bethune 1/40,000. Attack made on our left by the 142nd Infantry Brigade. A & C. Coys in Support reserve trenches respectively. Casualties:–
B. Coy. A/Cpl. Thomas. D. Killed in action Shot in neck.
D. Coy. A/Sgt. Bayh. F.J. – do –

Wednesday May 26th 1915 @ GIVENCHY (PONT FIXE)

B & D Coys in front line trenches till 4pm
A & C Coys in support Reserve respectively till 4pm
B & D Coys relieved by A & C Coys in front
line. B & D Coys falling back to Reserve &
support respectively, relief completed by 6pm.
Casualties this day include Major L J Oxley
"O.C" A Coy. Shell wound of back and arm.
One man killed & 7 & N.C.O's & four men
wounded through shell bursting near Cooks
Quarters at PONT FIXE. Shelter keeper killed
in trenches by S.H. Casualties as follows:—

B Coy - Capt James - A/a - No. 2044 Being Sunday
B Coy "   Morgan - to S/g No. 1534 (S.B.)
B Coy "   "   Field B/g No. 3160
A Coy "   "   Hitch - alt No. 396
B Coy "   "   Noorgood 6 No. 1321
B Coy Capt R/M/S Matthews a.f No. 616.

Thursday May 27th 1915 @ GIVENCHY (PONT FIXE)

A & C Coys in front line of trenches
D & B in Support Reserve respectively
14th Battalion came at 7pm & took over ½ batt
to supports. Very quiet all day. One casualty.
No. 2359 Pte Osborne. Shell wound of shoulder

Friday May 28th 1915 @ GIVENCHY (PONT FIXE)

A & C Coys in front line till 4pm. B & D Coys
in Reserve & support respectively. A & C Coys
relieved by B & D Coys in front line. A & C Coys
falling back to Support Reserve respectively.
Relief completed by 6pm. Very quiet all day.

Saturday May 29th 1915 @ GIVENCHY (PONT FIXE)

B & D Coys in front line. A & C Coys in
support Reserves respectively. Enemy shelled
PONT FIXE BRIDGE very heavily, one shell alighting
in a house where one platoon of 6 Coy were billeted
killing eight men and wounding five. Also
several others receiving slight injuries & shock.
Casualties as follows:—

Coy	Reg No	Rank & Name	S.K	Nature of Casualty	Remarks
C	2514	Pte Radmore J 8th		Killed in action @ GIVENCHY	All of these have except the last one killed
C	3012	" Willis a.E	do	do	Monday 24/5/15 @ PONT FIXE
C	2576	" Gordon F H	do	do	GIVENCHY
C	2561	" Abbott H.C	do	do	BETHUNE 24/5/15 @ PONT FIXE
C	2512	" Gordon R.C.	do	do	GIVENCHY.
C	363	" Boden L.E.	do	do	In Quotes all of
C	242	" Mann J.A.	do	do	last three all buried
C	1498	" Scholes W B	do	do	side by side
C	251	Pte Odell A		Wounded in action	All taken to 140th
C	3169	" James C.J.	do	GIVENCHY	
C	2035	" Moor S.C.	do	do	Some received Fiels Ambulence
C	1986	" Kaiger A.H.	do	do	
C	2205	Pte Watson C	do	do	

Sunday. May. 30th 1915 @ GIVENCHY (PONT FIXE).
B and D Companies in front line. A & C Coys in supports & Reserve respectively. Enemy shell PONT FIXE and a.H.Q very heavily during the day from 10.30 a.m. till 3.30 p.m. Sending over no fewer than 15 shells, one shell crashing into the entrance of H.Q. but luckily injuring no one. No Casualties.

Monday. May 31st 1915 @ GIVENCHY (PONT FIXE)
B and D Coys in front line till 4 p.m. A & C Coys in supports & Reserve respectively. B and D Coys relieved in the front line by A and C Coys. B Coy in support. D Coy in Reserves. Brigadier General Y.C. August Killed. Shot through Stomach at Sidney Monroe GIVENCHY about 4.30 a.m. Buried at BETHUNE 5.30 p.m. Officers & his men attended funeral. Commanding Officer attended. Commanding Officer take over Command of 141st Inf Bde (temporarily) from this date. Enemy open Shell PONT FIXE and H.Q. very heavily. A.C. Casualties. H.Q. Offices take over dug outs at ORCHARD FARM. Major Newman in Command while C.O. is away.

Tuesday. June 1st. 1915 @ GIVENCHY (PONT FIXE) & BETHUNE.
A & C Coys in front line open 3 Coy in support. D. Coy in Reserve till 8 p.m. PONT FIXE & H.Q. Shelled heavily during the early morning by Sergt Major of D Coy and 1 Man being injured. 1 Mule was also killed. Very quiet in front line up to time of relief. 5th & 10th Battalions Lahnadian Division relieve us about 8pm. Battalion in platoons by Companies march to BETHUNE via Dewes Road. and Marshall Bridge along the CANAL. to billets at Montmorency Barracks for one night. Casualties Officer. 2 Lieut G?Major Clark. G. No.34. 9 Coy 1955 Rfn Holmes I.R. Coy 533 Bugler Walker B. All three wounded by shell.

Wednesday June 2nd 1915 @ GIVENCHY (PONT FIXE, BETHUNE, & CAMBRIN
Wednesday. June. 2nd 1915 @ BETHUNE & CAMBRIN.
Battalion at BETHUNE till 4 p.m. Orders received to take over line at CAMBRIN relieving the Gloucester Regt. Battalion reach CAMBRIN and relieve Gloucesters about 9 p.m. B. C. and D. Companies in front line. A. Coy in support. H.Q. in trenches (dugouts) for first time. Very quiet. No casualties. New Brigadier takes over Command of 141st Inf Bde. (Lieut Thwaites from 4th Division) Commanding officer returns to Regiment.

Date	Entry	Casualties
9/3/15	Batt left St Albans for Southampton embarked S/S VIPER & TRAFFORD HALL.	
10/3/15	Disembarked at HAVRE.	
22/3/15	Battn inspected at HORONVILLE by Field Marshal Sir JOHN FRENCH.	
8/4/15	A & B Coys in FESTUBERT trenches.	One man wounded (B Coy)
9/4/15	C Coy — do —	2 OR wounded
14/4/15	D Coy — do —	1 OR killed 1 OR wounded
19/4/15	Batt took over trenches held by R.I. Fusiliers at LE PLANTIN	
23/4/15		2 OR wounded
23/4/15	LE PLANTIN.	1 OR wounded
24/4/15	Moved to GORRE.	1 OR D of W
27/4/15	LE PLANTIN	1 OR wounded
3/5/15	— do —	2 OR do
4/5/15	— do — & GORRE.	1 OR do
5/5/15	Moved to LA BEUVRIERE.	
8/5/15	— do — ESSARS Attached to 2nd Division	
9/5/15	Battn in First Army Reserve during attack on enemy lines. Evacuated billets at ESSARS & marched to LA TOURET.	
10/5/15	Battn took over new billets & H.Q at LA COUTURE. Battn still part of First Army Reserve.	
11/5/15	Battn moved Hd Qrs to E of LACON	
12/5/15	Moved to BEURY. New designation of 2nd Lon Div to 47th (Lon) Div. 5th Lon Inf Bde to 141 Inf Bde. Rejoined 47 Ln Div.	
13/5/15	Battn moved to GIVENCHY & took over line occupied by Camerons	
14/5/15	TRENCHES at GIVENCHY (Pont Fixe)	1 OR K.A 1 OR wounded
15/5/15	— do —	2 OR wounded
16/5/15	— do —	3 OR killed 4 OR wounded
17/5/15	— do —	1 OR killed 2 OR wounded
18/5/15	— do — Shelled pretty heavily nearly all night	1 OR wounded
19/5/15	— do — Shelling of Distillery, Canal Bank & Bridge at PONT FIXE	5 OR wounded
22/5/15	GIVENCHY PONT FIXE Heavy shelling by Germans.	No Casualties.

23/5/15	GIVENCHY	1 OR Killed 1 OR Wounded
24/5/15	do	1 OR K. 7 W.
25/5/15	do	2 OR K.A.
26/5/15	do	One Officer Wounded, 1 OR K.A. 5 OR wounded
27/5/15	do	One OR Wounded.

29/5/15 — do. Enemy shelled Pont FIXE Bridge. One shell hit house where one platoon of C Coy were billeted. 8 OR Killed 5 OR Wounded

30/5/15 GIVENCHY Heavy shelling. No Casualties.

31/5/15 — do — Brig. Gen. J. C. Nugent Killed. Comm. Officer taken over command of 141st Infy Bde (Temp) Major Newman in Command during C.O's absence.

1/6/15 GIVENCHY. Move to BETHUNE, shelled heavily during morning.   3. OR wounded.

2/6/15 BETHUNE & CAMBRIN. Took over line from Gloucester Regt. Col THWAITES 4th Div. took over command 141st Inf Bde. C.O. returned to Regiment.

3/6/15 CAMBRIN. Brigadier inspects Battn in firing line.

~~3/6/15~~ do & ANNEQUIN   1 OR wounded.

4/6/15 — do & ANNEQUIN. In Brigade Res. H.Q. shelled

5/6/15 ANNEQUIN. Enemy shelled village. 2 O.R. Killed

6/6/15 Marched to VERQUIN

7/6/15 VERQUIN. Proceeded by March Route to take over new billets at La PHILLOSOPHE

9/6/15 LE PHILLOSOPHE & FOSSE No 7. Relieved 19th Battn Lon Regt in trenches on BEUVRY-LENS ROAD.   1 OR Killed

10/6/15 FOSSE No 7. Capt H. D. Collison-Morley, taken over temporary Command of 19th Lon Regt. Capt F.C. Bawden taken over Adjutants duties of this Battn.   2 OR wounded

11/6/15 FOSSE No 7. in trenches   1 OR Killed

Thursday June 3rd. 1915 @ CAMBRIN.
B. C and D. Companies in front line. A Coy
in supports. Brigadier inspects Battalion
in firing line. Very quiet all day long.
Desultory artillery duels on our left. One Casualty
No. 3436. Rfn. Evans J. Shot through lip.

Friday June 4th. 1915 @ CAMBRIN and ANNEQUIN
B. C and D Companies in front line and A.
Company in Supports till 6pm. Battalion relieved
by 19th Battalion London Regt in front line Supports.
Battalion take up billets at ANNEQUIN in
Brigade Reserve. H.Q. shelled. Three
slight Casualties.

Saturday June. 5th 1915 @ ANNEQUIN
Battalion resting. Very quiet all day until about
4pm when the enemy shelled the village. Two
men of B. Coy Killed by Shell while walking
across field near Church. Casualties:-
A Coy. Rfn. Penfold. W.J. (3005) Killed by
B Coy. Rfn. Starr. A. (1148) Shell

Sunday June. 6th 1915 @ ANNEQUIN & VERQUIN
Battalion resting. Brigadier inspects Battalion
in supports. Brigadier inspects Battalion
in platoons outside billets. Orders received for
change of billets. Very quiet all day.
Heavy Bombardment takes place on our right.
Battalion marches off to new billets in platoons
at 50 yds interval between each platoon B Coy
leading at 11pm. March route via LA BASSÉE –
BEUVRY R.D. arriving at VERQUIN about 2am
4/6/15. Coys in billets and all Correct @ 3am.

Monday June 7th @ VERQUIN and LE PHILOSOPHE.
Battalion received orders to take over new billets
at LE PHILOSOPHE in Brigade Reserve.
Battalion march off from VERQUIN @ 8pm
arriving at their destination at 10pm.
Billets occupied and all Correct by 12 midnight.
March route

Tuesday June 8th. 1915 @ LE PHILOSOPHE.

Battalion in Brigade Reserve. Twenty four Officers commanding during the morning, the Battalion having to occupy there the Root Redoubt at FOSSE No.7. (Redt) torries and cupolas Very quiet all day.
No Casualties.

Wednesday June 9th. 1915 @ LE PHILOSOPHE AND FOSSE No.7.

Battalion in Brigade Reserve until 5 p.m. A/tk two trenches, which we are to occupy at FOSSE No.7, during the morning. Battalion relieve 19th Battalion London Regiment in trenches @ 8 p.m. on BEUVRY - LENS ROAD. Relief completed by 7 p.m. No. 1154. Pte. Casualties one. Emery W. (A)Coy. Shot through mouth. Killed. All quiet in our sector. Leave M. G. fire on our right.
A.Coy. left firing line Coy. B.Coy. Centre firing line Coy.
C.Coy. right firing line Coy. D.Coy. in Support.

Thursday June 10th 1915 @ E. of Village FOSSE No.7.

A.Coy. left firing line Coy. B.Coy. Centre firing line Coy.
C.Coy. right firing line Coy. Adjutant.
Capt. H. D. Bolton-Morley (The Buffs) goes to 19th Battalion London Regiment and takes temporary command. Capt. H. C. Bawden. O.C. D. Coy. takes over Adjutants duties of this Battalion.
Very quiet all day. Casualties two.
D.Coy. Rfn. Love. F. J. wounded in action (Head)
A.Coy. " Walden. H.   -do-   (nae.)
D.Coy in support in village

Friday June 11th 1915 @ E. of Village FOSSE No.7. S. of LE PHILOSOPHE.

A.Coy. left firing line Coy. B.Coy. Centre firing line Coy.
C.Coy. right firing line Coy. B.Coy relieved at 5 p.m. by D.Coy. who take over duties of firing line Coy. Commanding Officer attends meeting of 66th @ Brigade. Very quiet all day. Casualties na.
C.Coy. 2061. Rfn. Adams. R. J. Bullet across cheek. Relieved.
D.Coy in support in village until relieved by B.Coy.

Saturday June 12th 1915. @ Ed. VILLAGE Foss. No 7. S. of. LE PHILOSPHE. And

A. Coy left firing line Coy. D. Coy. centre firing line Coy. LE PHILOSOPHE.
C. Coy right firing line Coy. B. Coy in Reserve in village
Orders received to the effect that this Battalion to
attaches to 140th Inf Bde. and that we should be
relieved from the front line position that evening
Battalion relieved in front line at 8 p.m. by
4th. Batt. City of London Battalion. March to
billets A.B. Coy. and H.Q. in LE
PHILOSOPHE. B C & D. Companies in billets
at MAZINGARBE. Transport still @
HOUCHIN. Battalion in billets and all
correct at 2 a.m. next Morning

Sunday June 13th 1915. @ EA. PHILOSPHE & MAZINGARBE.

Battalion still attached to 140th Inf Bde and in
Brigade Reserve. Enemy shell very heavily
during the day. H.Q. and billets of A & B Coys
coming in for a bad time. Divine inspection
of Kit &c. carried out during the day.
Divine Services held this day by Mr Wood (C.E)
and Mr Atherton (N) Brigade Chaplains.
Casualties as follows:—

Coy.	Rank and Name.		Nature of Casualty.	Remarks.
A. 1355	Rfn	White F.	Killed by Shell. @ LE PHILOSOPHE	Buried Montchoday Irlam to 1412 and Jordon Irlam to Sola Ambulance
A. 3343	Rfn	Harris E.	Wounded in action by Shell at LE PHILOSOPHE	do
A. 2293	Rfn	Sala G.	do	do
A. 2088	Sgt.	Legg J.	do	do
A. 1082	Rfn	Hurst L.	do	do
A. 220	Rfn	Pitchfork J.	do	do
A. 4324	Rfn	Heath B.	do	do
A. 3344	Rfn	Weller Jn.	do	do
A. 3116	Rfn	Aldrick A.	do	do
A. 2473	Rfn	Taylor A.B.	do	do
A. 2691	Rfn	Carver J.	do	do
A. 3151	Rfn	Hagger J.C.	do	do
A. 1505	Rfn	Biggs F.A.	do	do
A. 2331	Rfn	Jones Jas.	do	do
A. 2242	Rfn	Sweeney J.	do	do
B. 323	Rfn	Boxall R. J.	Serious by wounded	do
A. 468	Rfn	Fish A.S.	do	do

The above were injured by two high explosive
shells. White and Boxall had already been
injured by one shell, but were back to rescue
some civilians

Monday June 14th 1915 @ LA PHILOSOPHE & MAZINGARBE.
Battalion still attached to 1140th Brigade and in Brigade Reserve. Enemy again shell LA PHILOSOPHE very heavily. No Casualties.

Tuesday June 15th 1915 @ LE PHILOSOPHE AND MAZINGARBE.
Battalion still attached to 1140th Inf Brigade and in Brigade Reserve. Enemy shell LA PHILOSOPHE very heavily. H.Q. Came in for a number of these owing to the fact that it had situated between two leary British batteries. No Casualties.

Wednesday June 16th 1915 @ LE PHILOSOPHE & MAZINGARBE.
Battalion still attached to 1140th Inf Brigade and in Brigade Reserve. Orders received for move to fresh billets at NOEUX-LES-MÊNES and 15th Batln for Regt to relieve us. This order cancelled and order received to be ready in half an hour to support the 1140th Inf Bde, an attack from the direction of LOOS being feared. Batln ready and move off at midnight to dug outs behind FOSSE No. 7. (N. LE PHILOSOPHE). Casualties Nil.

Thursday June 17th E. of VILLAGE, FOSSE No. 7, LE PHILOSOPHE.
Battalion in support of 1140th Inf Bde. 3 days out in rear of this FOSSE No. 7. Enemy aeroplane times trenching bombs on our dump. One hitting a dug out used for storing timber, pipes etc., and another hitting a belier belonging to one of our N.C.O's who had a narrow escape. The bolt itself being a petrol tank which spurted in all directions flaring petrol directly it touched the ground. N.C.O. No 760. Sgt. W.E. Bowles. D. Coy. this N.C.O's rifle burnt badly. Rifle supplied having 10th in magazine. No other Casualties. Battalion returns to billets at 10am. Orders received to move into new billets @ NOEUX-LES-MÊNES. Battalion relieved by 15th London Regiment @ 11 p.m. Billets handed over and batt leaves about 11.30 p.m. Batt now attached to 1141st Brigade again, march to NOEUX-LES-MÊNES, take over billets of 18th Inf Reg. All correct. 3.0 am. No other Casualties. Battalion in Divisional Reserve and liable to be ready in case of emergency to support the line in Div Area at 2 hrs notice.

Friday June 18th 1915 @ NOEUX-LES-MINES.
Battalion resting. Headquarters at the Mairie
Close order drill &c. Bombers Bayonetiers
under training. Casualties Nil.
N.B. Battalion in Divisional Reserve in constant
readiness for emergencies. F.C.M. of Foulkes A/Cpl No 2109.

Saturday June 19th 1915 @ NOEUX-LES-MINES
Battalion resting. Headquarters @ Mairie
Close order drill &c. Carried out. Bombers &
Bayonetiers under strict training
Casualties Nil. Battalion still in
Divisional and holding themselves in
Constant readiness to move at 2 hours
Notice in case of emergency. 141st Brigade
relieve 142nd Brigade in belie W. tomorrow night

Lieut A. White Rans attached on special leave of 5 days from 141st Brigade this date.

Sunday June 20th 1915 @ NOEUX-LES-MINES AND LES BREBIS.
Battalion in Divisional Reserve. Divine
Services held this day. R.am.C. band
142nd London Field Amb! attended to 1of Englands
drum head service for Brigade. This Battn
Marched out on Battalion Headquarters
Orders received to the effect that relief are

to take place between 141st Bde 2nd 142nd Bde
in W Section. This Battalion takes over
Villets of 21st Battalion in LES BREBIS.
Starting point road junctn L.13.C.H.q. N of
Rpte. main NOEUX-LES-MINES - LES BREBIS
Road. Battalion arrived @ LES-BREBIS about
10.30pm. Battalion now in Brigade
Reserve and in readiness to move in case
of emergency 3 hours by night 1 hour by day.

Monday June 21st 1915 @ LES BREBIS.
Battalion in a Brigade Reserve Company
Officers &c... town Support W. Section.
Inspection of billets &c by C.O.
Cpl drill &c... Carried out during the day. Working
Parties supplied by C. Coy. 2 platoons
of A. Coy. for work with french
and on W. Section. Casualties Nil.

Tuesday June 22nd. 1915 @ LES BREBIS.

Battalion in Brigade Reserve.

At 12.5am Enemy shelled Les Brebis with long range gun, reported to be 11.5cm. Six shells were put over two falling into the school where "D"Coy were billeting with disastrous results. One also fell near Qm Stores and Orderly Room, damage being done to surrounding wall & building, but not injuring anyone. Wireless attached to Church probable cause. Further two inspections in M.Action by Company Officers. Inspections of equipment Arms & carried out & further Casualties during the day. List of Casualties through shell fire as follows:-

Coy	Rank and Name	Reg. No.	Nature of Casualty	Remarks
D.	Cpl Woodley F.	1925	Killed in Action @ LES BREBIS by Shell.	Buried:- Mazengarbe Cemetery
D.	Pte Blake W.J.	2945	Killed in action @ LES BREBIS by Shell fire	Mazengarbe Cemetery
D.	Pte Yates W.	2919	Killed in action @ Shell fire @ LES BREBIS	NEAR: L.22. d.0.3.
D.	Pte Lafferty E.A.	1230	Killed in action by Shell fire @ LES BREBIS	Ref map BETHUNE 1/40,000

Coy	Reg No	Rank and Name	Nature of Casualty	Remarks
D.	1349	Pte Kennedy W.	Wounded in action @ LES BREBIS wound of wrist by Shell	Taken to 142nd London Field Ambulance
D.	3390	" Mead H.J.	Wounded in action @ LES BREBIS wound of Shoulder by Shell	
D.	2853	" Russell W.J.	Wounded in action @ LES BREBIS wound of face by Shell	
D.	2343	" Hale E.J.	Wounded in action @ LES BREBIS wound of left arm by Shell	
D.	1404	A/Cpl Bufrd H.	Wounded in action @ LES BREBIS wound from Telephone by Shell	
D.	2824	Pte Daley J.	Wounded in action @ LES BREBIS Fracture Femur by T arm by Shell	
D.	1954	" Fuller E.J.	Wounded in action @ LES BREBIS wound of Head by Shell	NEUX
D.	1552	" Green J.	Wounded in action @ LES BREBIS wound of right leg by Shell	LES
D.	533	Cpl Golden B.	Wounded in action @ LES BREBIS concussed by Shell	MINES.
D.	2489	Pte Clark E.G.	Wounded in action by Shell @ LES BREBIS. wound of neck	
D.	2521	" Gatward	Wounded in action by Shell @ LES BREBIS. wound of axilla	
D.	3308	" Back E.	Wounded in action by Shell @ LES BREBIS.	
D.	2119	A/Cpl Lambeth J.D.	Wounded in action by Shell @ LES BREBIS wound of Head	
D.	2591	Pte Matthews J.	Wounded in action by Shell @ LES BREBIS. wound both legs	
D.	1591	" Wright A.	Wounded in action by Shell wound of Shoulder Tight foot	
D.	1209	" Luse Q.E.	Wounded in action by Shell @ LES BREBIS. wound of Head & right leg	
D.	1921	" Patrick H.	Wounded in action by Shell @LES BREBIS. wound of Abdomen	
D.	1316	" Barnard Q.E.	Wounded in action by Shell @ LES BREBIS. wound of lower Jaw	
D.	2346	" Berry J.J.	Wounded in action by Shell @ LES BREBIS wound of hand	
D.	1664	" Cole E.J.	Wounded in action by Shell @ LES BREBIS wound of left foot	
D.	1908	" Line R.E.V.	Wounded in action @ LES BREBIS wound right foot	
D.	2504	" Beure J.	Wounded in action @ LES BREBIS by Shell wound of neck	
D.	2304	" Clark J.	Wounded in action by Shell @ LES BREBIS	
D.	2335	" Watland J.A.	Wounded in action by Shell @ LES BREBIS both eyes gone	
D.	244	" Bolasso S.	Wounded in action by Shell @ LES BREBIS wound of neck	
D.	2613	" Doe H.D.	Wounded in action by Shell @ LES BREBIS wound of buttock	

Wednesday June 23rd. 1915 @ LES BREBIS.

Battalion in Brigade Reserve. Inspection of Arms, Equipment &c. Carried out by Corps of Arms, Equipment &c. Carried out by Specialist. Tour of inspection of W Section by Section Officer and those who had not already done so. Very quiet all day. Casualties Nil. Working parties supplied by "B" Company for W. Section.

Thursday June 24th. 1915 @ LES BREBIS & BULLY GRENAY

Battalion in Brigade Reserve. Orders received to relieve 18th Battn London Regt in W Section. Relief start from LE BREBIS Church at 9pm by platoons, intervals of five minutes between platoons. D. Coy leading. D. Company left firing line leading. B. Company night firing Company. A. Company in line Company. A. Company in support B. Company in reserve. Line taken over and all correct about 11.30pm. 18th Battn. fall back to Bde Reserve. C.O. inspects the new firing line taken over. Casualties Nil.

Coy	Regt No	Rank & Name	Nature of Casualty	Remarks
D.	2645	Cpl Murdoch P.B.	Wounded in action @ L.E.B. BREBIS by Shell. Trench Leah	Taken to 142nd London Field Ambulance thence to NEOUX LES MINES HOSPITAL
D.	1804	L/Cpl Truelove J.A.	Wounded in action @ LES BREBIS by Shell	do
D.	3325	" Mead G.L.	Wounded in action @ LES BREBIS by Shell Chest Legs	do
D.	3156	" Lamer	Wounded in action @ LES BREBIS	do
D.	2944	" Dodd A.	Suffering from Shock by Shell Shock @ LES BREBIS	do
D.	1258	" Hallett	—do—	do
D.	2361	" Gray R.D.	—do—	do
D.	1539	L/Cpl Briggs A.	—do—	do
D.	1526	Pt Toney W.	—do—	—do— wounds
D.	3511	" Allen W.	—do—	—do—
D.	1919	" Lippett L.	—do—	—do—
D.	1050	" James D.A.	—do—	—do—
D.	2341	" Frost A.J.	—do—	—do—
D.	1858	" Standen E.J.	—do—	—do— Total Casualties
D.	909	" Hanne L.	—do—	—do—
D.	3418	" Harvey Les.	—do—	—do— 4. Rifles
C.	2941	" Sinclair R.	—do—	—do— 30. rounds
D.	1901	" Riggs W.	—do—	—do— 22. Shock
D.	1836	" Maris W.	—do—	—do— 56 Total
D.	1136	L/Cpl Humphreys J	—do—	—do—
D.	2442	Pt Bates S.	—do—	—do—
D.	2323	" Rogers A.J.	—do—	—do—
A.	1468	" Harris W.	—do—	—do—
D.	1502	" Brown A.G.	—do—	—do—
D.	1618	" Pilkington G.S.	—do—	—do—

Friday. June 25th 1915 @ BULLY-GRENAY.

Battalion in front line (W.Seaton). D.Coy. left firing line Coy. B.Coy right firing line Coy. A.Coy in support. C.Coy in reserve. H.Q. of Battalion in village. Day quiet all day. Casualties Nil.

Saturday. June 26th 1915 @ BULLY GRENAY.

Battalion in front line (W.Seaton) D.Coy left firing line Coy. B.Coy right firing line Coy. A.Coy in support. C.Coy in reserve. H.Q. in village. Enemy shell village with High Velocity Shells, also reserve trenches where "C" Coy were working. Causing 6 Casualties as follows:-

Coy	Reg No.	Name and Rank	Nature of Casualty	Remarks
C.	3086	Pte Jenkins. S.	Multiple shell wound of back.	Later E.W. and Brookfield Amb
C.	2168	Pte Pate. H.	Sell wound of scalp. Nervous Debility (severe)	- ditto -
C.	3382	Pte Ormes. A.	Shrapnel wound of forearm	- ditto -
C.	3068	Pte Austin. Wm.	Shell wound of thigh	- ditto -
C.	4605	Pte Connell. J.	Slight shell wound right foot and left calf.	- ditto -
C.	4442	Pte Moseley. E.G.	Shell wound in chest & left thigh.	- ditto -

Sunday. June 27th 1915 @ BULLY-GRENAY.

Battalion in front line. (W. Seaton) D. Coy. left firing line Coy. B.Coy right firing line Coy. A.Coy in support. C.Coy in reserve. H.Q. in village. Day very quiet all day. Casualties Nil. The village receive evacuation orders from French Authorities, and to be out of the village by 9pm following evening.

Monday. June 28th 1915 @ BULLY-GRENAY.

Battalion in front line (W. Seaton) D. Boy left firing line Coy. B. Coy right firing line Boy. A. Coy in support. C. Coy in reserve. H.Q. in village. Village shelled with high velocity Shells. Casualties Nil. Inhabitants busy all day Moving out.

Tuesday June 29th 1915 @ BULLY-GRENAY
Battalion in front line (W. Section) D. Coy left firing line Coy. B. Coy right firing line Coy. A. Coy in Support. C. Coy in reserve. H.Q. in the village.

New formation of First Army to take place, reorganised as follows:-

Indian Corps — 51st, LAHORE and MEERUT Divisions.
First Corps — 2nd, 7th and 9th Divisions.
Fourth Corps — 1st, 47th and 48th Divisions.

The 47th Division will continue to hold its present front and will come under the command of 4th CORPS on the morning of June 30th. Very quiet all day. Casualties NIL.

Wednesday June 30th 1915 @ BULLY-GRENAY
47th Division now in 4TH CORPS from this date. Commanded by Major General C.S.L. BARTER, C.V.O. C.B. Battalion in front line (W. Section). D. Coy left firing line Coy. B. Coy right firing line Coy. A. Coy Support. C. Coy reserve. H.Q. in the village. Very quiet all day. Casualties Nil.

Thursday July 1st 1915 @ BULLY-GRENAY
Battalion in front line (W. SECTION). D. Coy left firing line Coy. B. Coy right firing line Coy. A. Coy in support. C. Coy in reserve. H.Q. in the village. Village shelled with large Trench Mortars. Two Casualties during the day.

Relief to take place tomorrow evening. 2463 Pvt Siebert J. Bond had right thigh also 2445 Pte Clark O.H. Shot from hip / B. Coy.

Friday July 2nd 1915 @ BULLY-GRENAY
Battalion in front line (W. Section) D. Coy left firing line Coy. B. Coy right firing line Coy. A. Coy in Support. C. Coy in reserve. H.Q. in village up to 9pm. Relief takes place at 9pm starting from 1st H.Q. N.I. relieving Battalion 20th London Regiment. This Battalion goes into Brigade Reserve in SOUTH MAROC. H.Q. at No. 269. Relief Completed and billets by about 1.30 am. All dogs found wandering about in front line + in billets in reserve to be destroyed. No 1294 Pte Lawrence A.F. wounds himself with bayonet by accidentally catching his thigh. (A Coy). Very quiet all day. No further Casualties.

Saturday July 3rd 1915 @ SOUTH MAROC.

Battalion in Brigade Reserve, in billets in the village, and for duty as working parties. Each horse replaced by troops to have its own dugout, and each of these dugouts to be built by the occupants (troops). Dug outs started. Village shelled with high velocity shells. One casualty. (B Coy) No. 2442. Pte Bryett. Lost 20th Batt right scapula. Working parties of 1 Officer and 50 men for work on 13A. found by D. Coy and another of 3 Officers and 150 men in Trenches of 1 Officer and 50 men. Officers Lt. R.K. O'Brien. B Coy. 2/Lt. N.J.K. Smith. A Coy. 2/Lt. R.L. Carpenter. D. Coy. B. Coy. The last party for work on B. LINE. W. 3. No further casualties.

Letter received today from the Brigadier Genl. expressing his extreme satisfaction at the amount of work done by the Battalion during its recent tour of duty in the trenches.

Copy of letter as follows :— Confidential
To :— I/14th Battalion London Regt.

The Brigadier General desires that all ranks should be informed of his extreme satisfaction at the amount of work done by the Battalion during its recent tour of duty in the trenches, more particularly with the defence to the "B" line of defence.

He cannot speak too highly of the keenness and willing spirit shown by all ranks in the execution of a difficult and tiresome piece of work.

I am further to say that the Major General Commanding the Division desires to compliment the Battalion on the work done.

The Brigadier feels convinced that all ranks will respond readily to the next call that may be made upon them.

3rd July 1915.   (Sd) S.J. Lane Captain
Brigade Major
141st Infy Bde.

141st Infantry Brigade. No. B.M. 189.

The above letter copies and sent round to Officers Commanding Companies and specialist sections to be read to all ranks this day.

The original letter will be found in the War Diary Envelope.

Sunday July 4th 1915 @ SOUTH MAROC

Capt H A Caldwell

Battalion in Brigade Reserve. Dug outs for each billet under construction. Working party from D. Coy 1. Off. 50 men. reported that they were taken for work on 2/Lt W.3. by R.E. Guide this day instead of 13a. as arranged. Working parties sick. for tonight supplied by A. B. and D. Coys. Parties required 1. Officer 50 men for trench 13. a. 3. Officers. 150. men for "B" Line of W.5. Village shelled with high velocity shells. No Casualties.

Monday July 5th 1915 @ SOUTH MAROC.

Battalion in Brigade Reserve. Dug outs for each billet still under construction. 16. Coy. Supply 1. N.C.O. and 12 men for Bde. Dug out. Working parties as follows.
2. Officers. 100 men Trench. 13a.. 20 Officers
100 men B. LINE. W.3. 1. Officer 50 men
Trench 25. Supplied by all Companies.
Village shelled heavily about 5 pm. 14 heavy shells burst over, falling around the Main Gate entrance to the village. No Casualties.

Tuesday July 6th. 1915. @ SOUTH MAROC and MAZINGARBE.

Battalion in Brigade Reserve. Dug outs not completed being completed this day. Orders received for relief by the 8th Battalion and to take over billets of 4th Battalion London Regiment at MAZINGARBE. Battalion relieved about 11 pm by 4th Battn. London Regt. and march to their billets in MAZINGARBE. Route:—

All correct, Battn. H.Q. notified to Bde and billets taken over by about 2 am. 4/7/15. Brigade now in "Divisional Reserve. and liable to be called on for support ready in 2 hours by day and 1 hour by night. Very quiet all day. Casualties Nil.

Wednesday July 7th 1915 @ MAZINGARBE.
Battalion in Divisional Reserve. Close
order drill &c. Carried out. Bombers,
Res. M. Gunners &c. under Special
Training. Working Parties Supplied
550 men. Officers to work with the
3rd & 4th London Steve B. R.E. Enemy
Shell Mazingarbe slightly. Casualties Nil.
While Batt'n is in Div Reserve they are
to be ready in case of emergency. Phones
by day and 1 hour by night

Thursday July 8th 1915 @ MAZINGARBE.
Battalion in Divisional Reserve. Close
order drill &c. Carried out. M. Gunners
Bombers &c. under Special Training
Message received today through Division
Routine Orders from Lord Kitchener. Copy
as follows:-
Divisional Routine Order. No. 4114. dated 8/4/15.
The General Officer Comdg. has much pleasure in
complying with the personal instruction which he received
today from Field Marshall Lord Kitchener to

convey to the troops of the Division his gratification
with the good work which they are doing and his
assurance that it is fully appreciated at home
Very quiet all day. Casualties Nil.

Friday July 9th 1915 @ MAZINGARBE.
Battalion in Divisional Reserve.
Close order drill &c. Bombers, Res M.
Gunners &all other Special details
under training
Message received
today from Field Marshall Lord
Kitchener through Gen Sir Douglas Haig
Comndg 1st Army as follows:-
Headquarters 1st Army.
July 9th 1915.

(Copy)

General Sir Douglas Haig has much pleasure
in informing all ranks under his Command that
Lord Kitchener was greatly pleased with his
visit to the 1st Army yesterday.
Lord Kitchener was able to personally
express his admiration of the troops, not only
to Sir Douglas Haig but also to several
Corps, Divisional, Brigade, and Unit Commanders.

P.T.O

Saturday July 10th 1915 @ MAZINGARBE

Battalion in Divisional Reserve. Close order drill carried out. Coy Inspections etc. Bombers, Res. M. Gunners & all other Special details under training. Very quiet all day. Casualties NIL. Working Parties 600/900 men supplied for work with 3rd & 4th London RE.

Sunday July 11th 1915 @ MAZINGARBE

Battalion in Divisional Reserve. Voluntary Divine Services for all denominations during the morning. Work continued on dug outs. Route marches of about 3 mile under Company arrangements by Platoons. Route west of &d N - S. fine though MAZINGARBE. Very quiet all day. Casualties NIL.

To those Commanders, and to those troops of the 1st Army whom Lord Kitchener has not been able to see personally, he desires to send a message of his deep appreciation of their fine work in the trenches.

The Secretary of State for War wishes the troops to understand that, although Complimentary telegrams are not sent after each gallant action, their daily deeds are closely and earnestly watched, and very warmly appreciated by those in authority at home.

Steps are to be taken to ensure that this order reaches every Soldier in the 1st Army.

(Sd) P. E. F. Hobbs.
Major Genl.
D. A. & Q. M. G. 1st Army

Original Orders in War Diary Envelope.

The above read out on parade to every man. Working Parties supplied this day. 6 Officers 600 men from all Coys to work with 3rd & 4th London RE's. Very quiet all day. Casualties NIL.

Monday July 12th 1915 @ MAZINGARBE.
Battalion in Divisional Reserve.
Parade drill carried out before and after breakfast. Bombers & Machine gunners under Special training. Transport inspected by Brigadier. Working Parties (2 of 300 N.C.Os. Men & 6 Officers) for work with 3rd & 4th London R.E. Dug outs &c under Construction Continued. Following extract from Brigade Routine Orders received. (Copy) S.S. Transport.

The Brigadier was extremely satisfied with the turn out of the 1st Line Transport of Battalions at his inspection this morning. The transport has reached a very satisfactory standard, which must be maintained.

The order of merit in which the Condition of the Transport of the Battalions is as follows:—

17th Battn London Regt.
20th   —do—
18th   —do—
19th   —do—

The two first named were specially Satisfactory.
Very quiet all day Casualties NIL

─────────────────────────────

Tuesday July 13th 1915 @ MAZINGARBE.
Battalion in Divisional Reserve.
Inspection of Companies by Commanding Officer. Message received from Brigade Office with reference to further duty in the trenches dated. B.M. 335. 13/7/15 thus Cancelling the rest which had been arranged for this Division. Copy of letter as follows.

In Consequence of the 48th Div. probably leaving the 4th Army Corps in the very near future owing to a Contemplated reorganisation of the Army in France, the posting of this Division into Corps Reserve has had to be postponed; Consequently the 141st Infantry Brigade must again take its tour in the trenches.

The Brigadier is convinced that all ranks of the Brigade will meet a renewal of trench duty with that splendid Spirit and readiness for that duty which they have always shewn and always will shew.

He desires to impress upon Commanding Officers the urgent necessity that exists for the improvement of the route, more especially for the digging of shell proof shelters in all lines of defence.

A memorandum will be issued tomorrow detailing with the work required in the nature of its importance and the plan of carrying it out.

Inspection of Brigade Corps Reserve at the Evacuation of this tour of duty is likely.
Very quiet all day Casualties Nil

Wednesday July 14th 1915 @ MAZINGARBE AND
E. of VILLAGE. FOSSE N°7. S. of LE PHILOSOPHE.
Battalion in Divisional Reserve till 8pm.
Orders received re moving up into trenches
and taking over part of Sect. X. Sub section
X.2. FOSSE N°7. Move starts about 8pm
by platoons at intervals of not less than
30yds. Front line taken over and all
correct by about 11.30pm. A. Coy. Centre Coy.
D. Coy. left Coy. C. Coy. right Coy. B. Coy. in support.

Thursday July 15th 1915 @ E of VILLAGE FOSSE N°7.
S. of LE PHILOSOPHE. (x.2. Section)
A. Coy. Centre Coy. D. Coy. left Coy. C. Coy. right Lieut C.G.
Coy. B. Coy. in support trenches. Working Martin to
parties supplied for work on these trenches by Hospital
the 19th Battalion. Very quiet all day. sick
Casualties ONE wounded N°. 14400. Pte Smith A. "C" Coy

Friday July 16th 1915 @ E. of VILLAGE FOSSE N°7. South
of LE PHILOSOPHE. (X.2. Section)
A. Coy. Centre Coy. D. Coy. left Coy. C. Coy. right
Coy. B. Coy. in support in trenches.
Working Parties supplied by 19th London Regt.
also by our Coys in front line for wiring &c.
Very quiet all day. Casualties NIL

Saturday July 17th @ E of VILLAGE FOSSE N°7. SOUTH OF
LE PHILOSOPHE (X. Section Sub section X.2.)
A. Coy. Centre Coy. D. Coy. left Coy. C. Coy.
right Coy. B. Coy. in support in trenches.
Working Parties supplied for work on these trenches
by the 19th Battalion London Regt. Very quiet
all day. Pioneer section (newly formed body)
of 30 N.C.O's & Men of Skilled trades) on work in
trenches, Construction of dug outs etc.
Casualties NIL
B Coy change over with D Coy in centre.

Sunday. July. 18th 1915 @ E. of VILLAGE. FOSSE N°7.
SOUTH OF LE PHILOSOPHE. (X. Section. Sub Section. X.2.)

A. Coy Centre Coy. B. Coy. left Coy. C. Coy
right Coy. D. Coy in Support in trenches.
Working parties supplied by 19th Battn Jordan
Regt. and a party from Support Coy.
Pioneer section at work on dug outs.
Very quiet all day. Casualties. ONE.
Accidentally wounded in toe by careless use
of rifle. No 2030. Pr. Barnes. H. C. Coy.
Battalion relieved by 19th Coy left in X.2. Section
about 10 p.m, and to take over their billets
T.H.Q. in Brigade Reserve @ LE PHILOSOPHE
All correct by about midnight.

Monday July 19th 1915 @ LE PHILOSOPHE.
Working Parties supplied by us for work on X. Section
Sub Section X.2.
Parties supplied by. A < B. Companies.
Very quiet all day. ONE Casualty from
bombed with looking party. A. Coy. No 1333
A/Sgt Money. C. Shrapnel wound of Abd.
Battalion in Brigade Reserve in Constant
readiness to be called upon from by day 2 hour
by night if necessity arose

Tuesday. July. 20th 1915 @ LE PHILOSOPHE.
Battn in Brigade Reserve. Working
Parties supplied by all Corps day and night
Enemy shell very heavily during the day
On our right LES BREBIS was heavily shelled
during the Morning and our battery received
orders to fire on LENS. All Corps and Spec-
Sections were giving warning that all N.C.O's
+ Men not on duty were to Keep well
under cover.   Casualties NIL

Wednesday. July. 21st. 1915 @ LE PHILOSOPHE

Battn in Brigade Reserve. Working
Parties supplied by all Corps day and
night. Enemy again Shell
illage very heavily during the afternoon
Casualties wounded H.Q. Townsend Lee
Gunners Townsend Lee Bedis again
heavily.

Thursday July 22nd 1915 @ LE PHILOSOPHE.

Battalion in Brigade Reserve, working parties supplied by all Coys day and night. Enemy shell heavily Morning and afternoon. Batteries around us opened heavy fire and a right royal artillery duel took place. Major Keeman had a narrow escape in the early part of the morning, a piece of shell coming through the Mess Room window and just missing his head. A. Company Cookhouse shelled, and the following casualties resulted

ie. 2449. Pte Boice for. Multiple wds of hand & face.
 " 2619 " Denvir R. head. shrap frag.
 " 2081 " Bargar A. thigh.
 " 2070 " Woods W. -do-
 " 1740 " Long Jas. -do-
No other casualties

Friday July 23rd 1915 @ LE PHILOSOPHE & FOSSE No 7

Battalion leave Brigade Reserve and take over from 19th Batt London Regt. Relief complete and all correct about 11.30 pm. Brigade Sutherland Highlanders / Kitchener which in Reserve for intermediate stay with us for two same purpose for 8 tomoro. Platoons attached to Platoons, two of each company. Rest of Batts in local reserve in dug outs &c, very quiet all day with the exception of a few big signals. Commanding Officer came back from his eleven days leave to England this day. One platoon of the 47th (London) Divisional Cyclist Company also in Trenches when we arrived, are out tomorow night. Casualties Nil
Baths K.O.X.2. Quality street.

Saturday July 24th 1915 @ FOSSE No 7.
X Sector. Sub Sect X.2.

Batln in front line. Organis-
ational Highlanders (two platoons
from each coy) in trenches for instruction.
Divisional Cyclist Company (two platoons)
also in the trenches. Liquid smoke
Sutherland Highlanders relieved by
Battalion in local reserve, in
two companies from Yk Wings Own
Scottish Borderers, who came up
for instruction with this Battalion.
Platoons of Yk K.O.S.B's attached
to platoons of this Battalion in
front line. Rest of Battalion in
local reserve. Spent quiet all
day, with the exception of the
usual hrs bombardmnt. Nil.
Casualties this day Nil.
Battn H.Q. X.2. Quantity Inns

Sunday July 25th 1915 @ FOSSE No 7.
X Sector, Sub Section X.2.

Battalion in front line. Yk K.O.S.
B's attached to us for instruction
two platoons to each Platoon
attached to Platoons of this Batt.
& just two trenches. Rest of
Battalion in local reserve, in
dug outs around & we had
also one in the reserve line of
trenches. Devonshire Regimt
Coy Rey (two platoons) relieved
by two & one platoons of Shere-
wood Foresters. Relief complete no
casualty reported about about
8. John. Quiet by in the
trenches a few of Yk losses.
Full quiet all day long
both H.Q. X.2. Quantity Inns
casualties this day Nil.

Monday July 26th 1915 @ FOSSE No 7.
2nd Lieut Mick Sice. X.b.

Battalion in front line. Y.K.O.S.B's
attached for instruction in trench
warfare. Divisional quiet (enemy
trophies) who attacked one
casualty received in the watch of
the Kings Own Scottish Borderers
this day. No Relief complete and all
troops evacuated that were at.
being recently shot by a comrade
while cleaning his rifle. One
died later of wound. Very
quiet all day long. But
Bn Battalion in local reserve in
dug outs around time head and
also reserve trenches. (casualties
as before this Battn this day.
N.L.

Tuesday July 27th 1915 @ FOSSE No 7.
2nd Lieut Mick Sice X.b. and LE PHILOSOPHE

Battalion in front line. Y.K.O.S.B's
attached for instruction in trench warfare
Divisional quiet (enemy) also
trophies Very quiet all day. The
Battalion relieved by 14th Ledon
Regt. Relief complete and all
except as stand fast were at
10 a.m. Bath Gard by platoons
to LE PHILOSOPHE. into Brigade
Reserve. men in billets, all arrived
about mid-night. Casualties
this day. NIL.

Wednesday July 28th 1915 @ LE PHILOSOPHE
Battalion in Brigade Reserve. looking
Parties supplied (day and night) by
all Companies. Usual Shelling
of surrounding district today.
(Tuesday day) otherwise nothing
exciting happened. Casualties
NIL.

Thursday July 29th 1915 @ LE PHILOSOPHE.

Battalion in Brigade Reserve and in readiness to move at 2 hours notice by night and 1 hours notice by day.
Working parties supplied by all Companies during Night and Day. Quiet all day.
Casualties Nil.

Friday. July 30th 1915 @ LE PHILOSOPHE and SOUTH MAROC.

Battalion in Brigade Reserve up to 6pm. Orders received to attach ourselves to the 140th Inf Bde for two days in reserve in MAROC billets. Battalion Marched from LE PHILOSOPHE about 8pm and Marched via MAZINGARBE — LES BRÉBIS to SOUTH MAROC.
Battalion relieved and took over billets of 8th Sudan Regt, and all direct by Midnight.
Casualties Nil.

Saturday July 31st 1915 @ SOUTH MAROC. W. Sector.

Battalion attached to, and in reserve for 140th Infantry Brigade.
Working parties (day & night) supplied by all Companies. Very quiet all day.
Casualties Nil.

Sunday August 1st 1915 @ SOUTH MAROC and NOEUX-LES-MINES.

Battalion attached to, and in reserve for 140th Infantry Brigade in to Section.
Day Working parties supplied. Orders received to take over billets vacated by 18th Bn Regt @ NOEUX-LES-MINES. Battn relieved about Midnight by Seaforth Highlanders and Marched to LES BRÉBIS — MAZINGARBE NOEUX-LES-MINES Road to billets in NOEUX-LES-MINES.
Casualties this day Nil.

Monday August 2nd 1915 @ NEOUX-LES-MINES

Battalion arrive and all correct in billets about 2am. Battalion formed Divisional Reserve, and under 4 hours notice at Home ready by day, 1 hour at Home by day, in case of emergency. Orders of equipment, etc. carried out. The day was a cativities (?) at Battn H.Q. or on the move.

HALLICOURT – PLACE-A-BRAY – MARLES-LES-MINES. to ALLOUAGNE. Billets taken over and all correct about 10pm. Casualties Nil.

Tuesday August 3rd 1915 @ NEOUX-LES-MINES and ALLOUAGNE

Battalion in Divisional Reserve. Orders issued for move to fresh billets and to form Reserve at ALLOUAGNE. The arrangements first made were as follows:-
Move from NEOUX-LES-MINES at 4pm. march to HALLICOURT, bivouac with 18th, 19th and 20th Battalions as a Brigade and march to ALLOUAGNE via PLACE-A-BRAY, MARLES-LES-MINES these arrangements cancelled and the Battalion marched via

Wednesday August 4th 1915 @ ALLOUAGNE

Battn in Corps Reserve to 4th Corps. Inspection of all arms of the Battn by the Armourer Sergeants. Coy Inspections carried out with regard to following Smoke helmets, Respirators, Equipment, Clothing, Battn Boots during the afternoon. A. Battalion sing Song arranged on the Battn Parade Ground which beat off very successfully. Transport Inspection by Commanding Officer. Casualties this day Nil.

Thursday August 5th 1915 @ ALLOUAGNE

Battalion in Corps Reserve for 4th Corps.
Company training carried out.
Including Physical Exercises and
Running drill. Lieut W.S. MACK.
reports to duty and is taken on
Strength of Battalion from this date.
Battalion carried out fore part Bath.
Casualties this day Nil —

Friday August 6th 1915 @ ALLOUAGNE

Battalion in Corps Reserve for 4th Corps.
Company training carried out.
Inspections under Coy arrangements.
Iron Rations, Rifle Slings, Identity discs
Early Morning Physical Exercises and
Running drill.
Bathing being arranged and takes
place on Battn Parade Ground
Casualties this day Nil —

Saturday August 7th 1915 @ ALLOUAGNE

Battalion in Corps Reserve for 4th Corps.
Company training carried out consisting of
Close Order drill, Extended Order drill,
Musketry, &c.
Specialists took work under own Officers.
Commanding Officer inspected the
Battalion by Companies in the
afternoon, Commencing with B Coy.
Casualties this day Nil —

Sunday August 8th 1915 @ ALLOUAGNE

Battalion in Corps Reserve for 4th Corps.
Divine Services for all denominations
arranged.
Church of England service takes place behind
Brigade H.Q. under Brigade arrangements.
Both Officers and Men attend for the C.E.
(Drum head service) conducted by
Rev. C.I.S. Woods, Chaplain to Brigade.
Chaplains this day Nil —
Casualties this day Nil —

Monday. August 9th 1915 @ ALLOUAGNE

Battalion in Corps Reserve for 4th Corps.
Programme of work this day as follows:-
Coy. Order Drill Ceremonial under
Batt. Arrangements. Running drill
and Physical exercise early morning
under Company arrangements.
Battalion School of Instructors organised
and begins to day. Organised
for the purpose of training Young
Officers, N.C.O.s of the 1 Battn.
Class consists of 3 Off. 14 N.C.Os = 20 in
all. Officers:– 2/Lt. T.L. CATER.
2/Lt. C.G. HATCH. and 1/T (Temp) W.S. HACK(?)
Specialists Came under Supervision
and work seperately from Batt.
M. Gun Instrs. Grenadiers. S.A. Batty.
Grenadier Officer { W.A. CLARKE.
                  { H.J. WITHERS.
M. Gun   do   { R.D. ROBB.
Company Officers arrange Lectures on
subjects & Intelecto to give them, to the men
in the evening for 1 hour.
Casualties. Nil ~ day. Nil ~

Tuesday. August 10th 1915 @ ALLOUAGNE

Battalion in Corps Reserve for 4th Corps
@ ALLOUAGNE took this day as follows:-
Training this day under Company
arrangements
Casualties this day. Nil ~

Wednesday. August 11th 1915 @ ALLOUAGNE

Battalion in Corps Reserve for 4th Corps.
Training Events of:– Battalion Drill.
Ceremonial & close order Drill.
Parties in the afternoon under Conft.
Arrangements. Specialists both
the Brigade under own officers.
Casualties this day. Nil ~

Sunday August 12. 1915 @ ALLOUAGNE

Battalion in Corps Reserve for 11th Corps.
Route march for Battalion as follows:—
ALLOUAGNE – BURBURE – BURBURE-LILLERS Road
X Roads. O.14.a. 2.4. and O.14.b. 6.0.
thence via LILLERS – ALLOUAGNE. LILLERS Road
to ALLOUAGNE. Starting point X Roads
O.14. a. 1.4. (Ref Map. BETHUNE. 1/40,000.)
Casualties this day Nil

Friday August 13th 1915. @ ALLOUAGNE

Battalion in Corps Reserve for 11th Corps

Musketry trained men & recruits carried out the
Trained men on Range X. O.29. a. o. Ref Sheet 36.2.
day.
Recruits on " Y. D.14. c. 9.9. – do – 36.4.
Battalion School of Instruction for Officers
N.C.O's. Company training for those
not on range. Specialists under Brigade
and own Officers. Casualties Nil

Saturday. August 14th 1915. @ ALLOUAGNE

Battalion in Corps Reserve for 11th Corps.
Battalion Drill – Ceremonial Close Order Drill
Battalion School of Instruction
Specialists under Brigade (numerous carried
out training according to arrangements

The afternoon was set aside for Battalion sports
which had been arranged by Sports Committee
Major S.F. was President. R.S.T. Tournée Secretary.
Secretary. It was arranged that all
winners should represent Battalion in
Brigade Sports
Programme as follows:—

    1 —   100 yards.
    2 —   80 yards
    3 —   1 Mile relay race (teams of four)
    4 —   120 yards Officers Canteen
    5 —   Inter Battalion Tug of war.
          (Catch weight - teams of eight)
    6 —   1 Mile
    7 —   Pick a back tourney
    8 —   High jump
    9 —   440 yards

Sunday August 15th 1915 @ ALLOUAGNE

Battalion in Brigade Reserve for 14th Corps.
Commanding Officer of the Battalion i.e.
(Lieut Colonel James Godding) takes over
Temporary Command of the 114th
Infantry Brigade from this date.
Major W. W. Newman 2nd in Command
of this Batta. takes over Command
Temporary during Colonel's absence.
Divine Service held this day.
Church of England drum head service
Relia Bole N.G. in field. 30 men
100 men from each Coy attended
Service Conducted by the Brigade
Chaplain. Rev. C. V. Wood. (Capt)
14th Inf Bde attended with Staff Captain.
All Officers who were not on other duties
and leave were present.
To training of any kind take
place this day.
A Concert was arranged for the evening
and took place at 7 pm.
Casualties this day NIL

Saturday August 14th 1915 (continued)
Sports (Events Returned)
10. Long Jump
11. Costume Race.
12. Sergeants Foot Race.
13. Sack race.

Day of how pulls all over.
All gates to the men to service trousers and
boots.
The band was in attendance, and
afforded much amusement by the Cateness
in which they turned out in.

Commanding Officers who were A/Brigadiers of
114th Inf Bde attended with Staff Captain.
All Officers who were not on other duties
and leave were present.
A Concert was arranged for the evening
and took place at 7 pm.

The whole afternoon and evenings entertainment
was in every way a success, and everyone
was satisfied with arrangements which were made
by the Quartermaster Lt. G. T. Townsend, with help of
Committee.
Casualties this day NIL

Monday. August. 16th 1915 @ ALLOUAGNE

Battalion in Corps Reserve for 4th Corps.
Running Drill & Physical Exercises carried out (early morning). Battalion Drill & Ceremonial. Company Training Commenced.
Specialist under Specialists Commenced.
Battalion School of Instruction.
Bathing &c.. Musketry.
Casualties this day. Nil.

Tuesday. August. 14th 1915 @ ALLOUAGNE

Battalion in Corps Reserve for 4th Corps.
Running Drill & Physical Exercises carried out (early morning). Battn Drill & Ceremonial. Specialist under Brigade Orders & under Specialists Commanders. Brigade Sports held in the afternoon in field adjoining 20th Battn H.Q.
Events won by this Batts were as follows:-
100 yards race (2nd Prize)
Battn inter-coy Pack Mule (—do—)
Post time Obstacle Race (1st Prize)
Long Jump (2nd Prize)
Bombing Race (1st Prize)

Sports (Brigade continued).

Sports held here very successful and many here in attendance.
A Concert in which all Battalion took part was arranged & commenced at 4 p.m. This also was a huge success, thanks to organisers.
Casualties this day. Nil.
Orders received to move next day to HOUCHIN and to bivouac.

Wednesday. August. 18th 1915 @ ALLOUAGNE and HOUCHIN.

Battalion in Corps Reserve for 4th Corps.
Battn prepare to evacuate billets and got ready for moving 13pm. Orders to the effect that the 142nd Infantry Brigade to go to HOUCHIN to carry out entrenching work and to find working parties for the GRENAY line if required. We were the Battalion selected to bivouac. Rest of Brigade to take up billets in the village of HOUCHIN.
Battalion leave ALLOUAGNE, about 1pm in

two parties. 1st party under command of Major. F.E: EVANS. 2nd Party under command of MAJOR. T.G.W. NEWMAN (Company in command of Battn.) Band marched with 1st party half way and then picked up 2nd party for the rest of the journey.

ROUTE:- ALLOUAGNE -
LAPUGNOY. - PLACE-A-BRAY - HOUCHIN
VILLAGE. to bivouac just on back of HOUCHIN.

Transport experienced great difficulties during the march. Route took them through a wood just the other side of LAPUGNOY and what with head to the depth of at least 2in. 3ft. and very steep hills at frequent intervals, the journey was much longer than anticipated. Many times they got fast held in the mud, slime and Cordé only removed with the help of men from the tanks. Eventually transport wearicades in getting through wood, and arrived at HOUCHIN 4 hours late. Rest of Battn. arrived at 9am and took over bivouacs evacuated by London Regt. who went to ALLOUAGNE in billets quite this day. (casualties this day Nil.

Thursday. August 19th 1915 @ HOUCHIN.
(in bivouacs in wood).

Battn. in Corps Reserve for 4th Corps.
Working Parties found by this Battalion for work on GRENAY line of defence.
Two reliefs:- 1st party A & B Companies
6.30 a.m to 12. 30 p.m. 2nd Party
B-D. Companies 12.30 pm. to 6.30 P.m
Parties not worried by enemy.
Casualties Nil.

Friday. August 20th 1915 @ HOUCHIN
(in bivouacs in wood)

Battn. in Corps Reserve for 4th Corps.
Working parties found for GRENAY line of defence.
1st party. 6.30 am to 12.30 pm
2nd party 12.30 pm to 6.30 pm
Parties not worried by enemy.
Casualties Nil.

Saturday August 21st. 1915 @ HOUCHIN.
(In bivouacs in wood.)

Battalion in Corps Reserve for 4th Corps.
Working parties supplied for work on GRENAY.
line of defence.
1st. Party :-   6.30 am to 12.30 pm.
2nd Party :-   12.30 pm to 6.30 pm.
Working Parties not worried by enemy.
Casualties this day NIL.

Sunday August. 22nd 1915 @ HOUCHIN.
(In bivouacs in wood)

Battalion in Corps Reserve for 4th Corps.
Working parties supplied for work on GRENAY.
line of defence
1st Party :-   6.30 am to 12.30 pm
2nd Party :- 12.30 pm to 6.30 pm.
Working parties not worried by enemy. Casualties Nil.
Guards Platoon attached to Brigade during stay
at HOUCHIN. Voluntary services held this
day. All denominations

Monday. August 23rd. 1915 @ HOUCHIN.
(In bivouacs in wood.)

Battalion in Corps Reserve for 4th Corps.
Working parties supplied for work on GRENAY line
of defence.
1st Party :-   6.30 am to 12.30 pm
2nd Party :- 12.30 pm to 6.30 pm
Working parties not worried by enemy.
Casualties this day NIL.
Adjutant attends Course of Bombing at
School of Instruction held @ LABEUVRIERE.

Tuesday August 24th. 1915 @ HOUCHIN.
(In bivouacs in wood)

Battalion in Corps Reserve for 4th Corps.
Working parties supplied for work on GRENAY line
of defence.
1st Party :-   6.30 am to 12.30 pm
2nd Party :- 12.30 pm to 6.30 pm
Working parties not worried by enemy. Casualties Nil.
Adjutant attends Course of Bombing at School
of Instruction held @ LABEUVRIERE.

Tuesday August 24th 1915 @ HOUCHIN
(In bivouacs in wood). (Continued).

Battalion &c (Companies not on duty) spent afternoon viewing Cricket match between Officers & 60th Rifles. Very interesting and exciting afternoons play.
Casualties this day NIL.

Wednesday August 25th 1915 @ HOUCHIN
(In bivouacs in wood) and LES BREBIS.

Battalion in Corps Reserve for 4th Corps. Battalion free, with the exception of any emergency that should arise, till moving off in the evening. The morning included an interesting Cricket match which was arranged and which drew off very successfully. Cricket Match was between Teams, one composed of Officers, and the other of No 6's & 7's of the Battalion. (12 per side.) Very exciting & interesting, and same good sport resulted.   Result NIL

Captain A.S. Hands to hospital this day sick.

Battalion moves from bivouac at HOUCHIN and marches in platoons at 300 yards intervals via
NOEUX-LES-MINES – MAZINGARBE – LES BREBIS.
Arrive at LES BREBIS about 9 p.m. Billets taken over and reported all correct at 10 p.m.
Casualties this day NIL.

Thursday August 26th 1915 @ LES BREBIS.

Battn in Corps Reserve for 4th Corps.
Battn digging on GRENAY line of defence under orders of O.C. 25th Army Troops Coy.
Parties supplied as follows:–
First party:–   A – 6. to 6. a.m. – 3 p.m.
Second party:– B – 2. to 8 p.m. – 3 a.m. 24/8/15.

It must be noted that the following Special Sections here at HOUCHIN having been left behind for training under Brigade orders.
M. Gun (Standing, 1st Reserve & 2nd Reserve &c.)
Grenadiers (– do – 1st Reserve Platoons)
Sniping (– do – Section)
In Batty.
We could only train with every available man working parties of about 400 all ranks.
Casualties NIL

Friday. August 24th. 1915 @ LES BRERS

Battalion in Corps Reserve for 4th Corps.
Battalion supply working parties to EPENAY
line of defence under orders of O.C.
25th Army Troops Company.
Parties supplied as follows:-
A and C Companies from 6am to 3pm
B and D Companies from 3pm to ?
Working parties not worried by enemy
in and had
Casualties this day — Nil

Saturday August 25th 1915 @ LES BREPS

Battalion in Corps Reserve for 4th Corps.
Battalion supply working party in which
whole Battalion forms the body.
Took whole out at night under
orders of 1140 Infantry Brigade.
Engaged on digging saps and a
new front line connecting left of W.2.
with Quarry. Average 300 yards

in front of existing firing line.
Work stopping. N. kind of line.
Very moonlight night but men say
silent and though between 200 &
250 yards from German front line
working party were not worried

Casualties — Nil

Sunday, August 29th 1915 @ LES BREPS

Battalion in Corps Reserve for 4th Corps.
Battalion supply working party (Officers
A.B.C.D. Coys two Officers each with Brigade &
HOUCHIN) for night work on EPENAY line of
defence. Orders as of 14th Aug Bie.
Not came as yesterday.
Very moonlight night parties not worried
by enemy. Suday Coys Place & hour
of ?

Casualties — Nil

Monday. August 30th 1915 @ LES BREBIS.

Battalion in Corps Reserve for 4th Corps.
Battn supply working party. (Un four parte A.B.C.D. Companies two Subaltern
& two men Brigade Orders @ HOUCHIN,
in all about 400 all ranks). BRENAY line of defence
Work done as two days previous.
Very moonlight night. parties NOT
seen by enemy.
Casualties — NIL —
Congratulatory message received today
though Brigade from G.O.C. 47th (London)
Division on work accomplished by
Battalion during the last two weeks
on this special portion of the line.
Orders received by C.O. to move
Bttn back to HOUCHIN by motor buses
after Packs had stacked up at Battn
H.Q. and all billets left clean
& correct by 8pm. looking forward
since Les Brebis for work on front line
by 9pm.

Tuesday. August 31st @ HOUCHIN.

Battalion in Corps Reserve for 4th Corps.
Battalion finish work on the BRENAY line
of defence about 2am, march to
LES BREBIS take up packs already
stored @ Battn H.Q. and proceed
to motor buses for HOUCHIN.
Journey via NOEUX-LES-MINE —
MAZINGARBE ROAD — NOEUX-LES-MINES —
to HOUCHIN arriving about 3.30am.
Billets had already been arranged
and after breakfast which had
been got ready troops turned
in for sleep. Reveille for
Batt" during time working parties
was 11 a.m. Inspection
of equipment, arms, Gas
pro., carried out this day by
C. coys. Demonstration lecture
@ Brigade Bombing School by performers
of Gas and the use of
smoke helmets. Officers attended.
Weather today hot
night successful. E.O. Lott.

the Officers & other Ranks passed through trench in single file, this similar to trench that the Germans had used was turned on from a cylinder, and the trench flooded. Shell holes had been carefully but now before entering trench. Small holes that proved its value and no casualties occurred.

Casualties during the day — Nil.

Wednesday September 1st 1915 @ HOUCHIN.

Battalion in Bgde Reserve for 4th Corps. Company Training carried on during the morning. — Inspection of Cattle by Brigadier General Hunter in the afternoon. Ceremonial Parade.

Turn out very successful.

Casualties this day — Nil.

Thursday September 2nd 1915 @ HOUCHIN.

Battalion in Bgde Reserve for 4th Corps. Batts. Practice an attack across Country during the morning. Enemy troops arrive home chuckled. Inspection of Equipment Smoke Helmets and Ammunition Quantity docs. Iron Rations Rifle Side Arms Gas Sc, by OC Corps.

Casualties this day — Nil.

Friday September 3rd 1915 @ HOUCHIN.

Battalion in Bgde Reserve for 4th Corps. Batts. practised another attack scene as day before in the morning. Company Training during the afternoon.

Casualties this day — Nil.

Saturday September 4th 1915 @ HOUCHIN and LES BREBIS

Battalion in Corps Reserve for 1st H.Q.Ops. Battalion carrying out Battle-training during the morning. Battalion orders as per Diary. Preparing to move and supply Working Parties today, uncertainty existed up to 4 p.m. although billeting parties had hurried away in many billets.

Move confirmed and Battalion move by Motor bus to LES-BREBIS via NOEUX-LES-MINES and NOEUX-LES-MINES - MAZINGARBE road to LES BREBIS Church where H.Q. and P.M. STORES (School) Remd. to front line on disembark and after stacking up packs @ Company for working party on ERNAY trenches in front of existing front line of defence took canned out as follows:- line at NAHAOE. W.3. dodders. Lunches in front of existing front

---

Sunday September 5th 1915 @ LES BREBIS

Battn in Corps Reserve for 1st H.Q.Ops. Battn on took on front line in fact of existing fully line (A.B.C.D.) Itparties supplied and took under orders of R.E. took for 8th and all Bns.

Casualties Nil

Monday September 6th 1915 @ LES BREBIS and NOEUX-LES-MINES Battalion rests

In Corps Reserve for 1st H.Q.Ops. Casualties Nil

Tuesday September 7th @ NOEUX-LES-MINES
Wednesday " " 8th " — 3 days

under Captain Bobbies proceeds on the evening of the 8th to billets in LES BREBIS and finds day working parties for work at MAROC, on 9th 10th and 11th, returning to NOEUX on the evening of the 11th. Casualties Nil

Sunday. September 12th @ NOEUX-LES-MINES
and LES BREBIS   Capt
                                            R.J. Davids
Battn in Corps Reserve for 4th Corps.   to hospital
Move by buses to LES BREBIS and   sick.
works night 12th/13th on front line W.3.
Sector.

Monday 13th September 1915 @ LES BREBIS.

Battalion in Corps Reserve for 4th Corps.
Officers informed of impending operations
and proceed to observing station for
reconnaissance. Battn works night
13th/14th on front line W.3. Sector

Tuesday. September 14th 1915 @ LES BREBIS.

Battalion in Corps Reserve for 4th Corps.
Battalion works night 14th/15th on front
line W.3 Sector and returns by bus to
HOUCHIN.
  Casualties this day Nil

Wednesday September 15th 1915 @ HOUCHIN.

Battn resting, resting and cleaning
up.
  Battn in Corps Reserve for 4th Corps
  Casualties this day Nil.

Thursday. September 16th 1915 @ HOUCHIN

Battalion training.
3 Companies under Major F.E. Brown
proceed to LES BREBIS and works
by day on Brigade fighting H.Q.
etc. N. MAROC. Lt. Col. Major Jeffries
Newman receives orders to take over temporary command
of the 23rd Battn London Regiment. Casualties Nil

Friday September 17th 1915 @ HOUCHIN.

Battn Corps Reserve for 4th Corps.
Major Brown's party in trenches W.3. Sector.
Heavy Shelling by enemy. One heavy
armour piercing Shell struck Shelter
in which a platoon of D Company
was taking Cover.
  Casualties overleaf

Saturday September 18th 1915 @ HOUCHIN.

Working party under Major L.E. Evans returned in the evening.

Sunday. September. 19th 1915 @ HOUCHIN.

Battn in Corps Reserve for 4th Corps.
Church Parade & all details of Brigade @ HOUCHIN.

Afternoon. All officers attended demonstration of Smoke bombs &c., just South W! of HOUCHIN. HILL.
Divisional General and Staff with Several Senior Generals present.

Casualties this day – NIL

Monday, September 20th 1915 @ HOUCHIN.

Battn.

Battalion training 8am to 7.30pm.
Col. 1st Bn. Bde present throughout.
Major T.S. Lamonier resumes
Orders to take over command of
2nd Battn London Regiment.

Tuesday. September 21st. 1915 @

Monday September 20th 1915 @ HOUCHIN.

Company Training. New Battn.
Flag presented by Lieut Col. his Lordship
dedicated by Brigade Chaplain,
Rev. C.S.S. Wood. Short impressive
service and inspiriting address to troops
Battalion moves by buses to Lillers
@ LES BREBIS. and works night 20/21 St.
Casualties Nil.

Tuesday. September 21st 1915 @ LES BREBIS.

Battn rest during the day and works
night 21/22nd.
Commanding Officer and Adjutant
attend final conference on operations
at Brigade Office. NOEUX-LES-MINES
and receive operation orders.

Wednesday September 22nd 1915 @ LES BREBIS.

Battn. resting. Wk's night 22nd/23rd.
Officers and N.C.O.'s continue reconnaissance of positions LOOS and Surroundings from W. "3" Sector.
Battn. Operation Orders issued and Conference of Officers called for the next day.

Casualties NIL

Thursday September 23rd 1915 @ LES BREBIS.

Final Conference of Officers and Completion of arrangements for operations.
Battalion takes over Sub. Sector W.3. from 23rd London Regiment as follows:—
A Coy right Company.
C Coy centre Company.
D Coy left Company including Sep. 18.
from 15th Division
May in reserve billets in N. MAROC.

Casualties NIL

Friday September 24th 1915 @ LES BREBIS.

Battn. in trenches. W.3. Sector.
Brigade H.Q. moves to Fighting H.Q. N. MAROC.

Casualties NIL

Saturday 25th September 1915 @ N. MAROC.

18

12.30 am   All Companies in New Front Line W.3. Sector withdrawn to original front line and disposed in dug outs 18th 19th and 20th Battn London Regt. form up for the attack. 19th Battn in Brigade Reserve and responsible for defense of W.3. Sector including LONDON ROAD KEEP. Manned by 1 Platoon, 4th Royal Welch Fusiliers

5.50 am.   Smoke and Gas Attack commences.

6.30 am   18th Battalion launches attack. Objective German Second Line Trenches

Saturday 25th September 1915. (continued):

followed by 20th Battalion objective Garden City and Chalk Pit East of LOOS. 19th Batt. objective "South Jones" LOOS.

4.0. a.m. Batt. H.Q. moves to advanced dug out East face of trench 26.

B Company. Commences forming up Sap. 18. with Old German Sap. and 13 toy Commences trench alongside GRENAY BENEFONTAINE. ROAD.

9.0. A. am. C Company and remainder LE. trans. ordered forward to reinforce 20th Battalion.

10.0. am. Remainder of Battalion relieved by the 23rd Batt. London Regiment and proceeds to German Second Line trench then held by 18th London Regt. Immediately on arrival A Company was ordered

Saturday 25th September 1915 (continued)

forward to reinforce 19th Batt. London Regiment and D. Company and to reinforce 20th Battalion.

2 Machine Guns moved under Lieut. to Robb to reinforce 20th Battalion

B. Company with 2 machine guns and Reserve Grenadiers were disposed in German Communication trench from German Second Line to Garden City.

About 5.0. p.m. two Companies East Yorks Regt moved in extended order from direction of VERMELLES across front in a South Easterly direction. It was not clear what they here doing and a large number of them ultimately came to the trench occupied by this Battalion and were taken Command of by Commanding Officer of this Batt. — Lieut Col Jno Godchuy.

Main Casualties this day. Captain W.R. Batters wounded in the heel by shrapnel. Lieut Shuffatt bullet wound in elbow. night uneventful.

Sunday September 26th 1915

Morning uneventful. Some shelling by the enemy.

During the afternoon frequent reports were received of retirement of troops on our left. About 5.0 p.m. owing to retirement of troops on the left, a retirement of the Brigade was ordered which took place to the German Second Line. Almost immediately however situation was such that all the positions previously held by the Brigade were reoccupied and held successfully throughout the night. Two regiments of Cavalry and part of the Guards Division attacked on the left. During the retirement of the Brigade Lieut. W.A. Percy was killed whilst steadying and rallying the men.

Officer casualties this day:
Lieut. J.D. Ross
Lieut. H.M. Clarke } Killed
Lieut. W.A. Percy

Sunday September 26th 1915

Maj. F.E. Evans. Gassed & Slightly wounded.
2/Lieut. G.J. Hatch. wounded.

Monday September 27th 1915

Attack on the Copse by a Company of the 2nd London Regiment and Grenadiers of the 1st & 2nd Brigade under command of Lieut Col Kubbatt of 2nd Bn perhaps. Attack not successful. Casualties small. Grenadiers of this Battalion under Lieut. W.R.Clarke did especially light unsuccessful post work.

Casualties during the operations 25/26 inclusive appended on separate sheet

Tuesday September 28th 1915.

Enemy Artillery active causing some casualties, otherwise the day uneventful. Brigade relieved by 142nd Inf Brigade. This Battalion ordered to occupy W.3. Sector. B, C, & D Companies in trenches. A Company in reserve billets in N. MARC. L. Machine Guns under Lieut. N.R. Smith attached to 22nd Batln Ln Regt. Relief completed about 2.0. a.m. 29th inst.

Casualties this day :- NIL.

Wednesday September 29th 1915. Batln in trenches W. 3. Sector.

Reinforcement of 92. N.CO's & Men arrive from Base.

Thursday. September 30th 1915.

Battalion relieves 1st London Regt in German Second Line trenches. Trenches heavily shelled and all men except look outs kept in dug outs. No Casualties.

Friday October 1st 1915.

Battalion relieved by 68th Regiment, French Infantry. 9.0. p.m. When to rendezvous provided, moving off to billets @ VAUDRICOURT where hot meals are about 2.0. a.m.

Casualties this day :- NIL.

Saturday October 2nd 1915 @ VAUDRICOURT.

Lieut Col H. Golding having been in bad health for some time decides to ask to be relieved of his Command. G.O.C. Brigade appoints Major E.H. Norman Royal West Kent Regiment late Adjutant of the 20th Battn London Regiment to the Command.

Casualties this day :- NIL.

Sunday. October 3rd. 1915 @ VAUDRICOURT and HESDIGNEUL.

Brigade Church Parade at which G.O.C. Division and staff were present. G.O.C. Division addresses and compliments the Brigade on its work. G.O.C. Brigade addresses and compliments the Battalion making reference to the very fine work done by Lieut Col. Fodding during the past year, and previously. Lt Col. J. Fodding bids farewell to the Battalion in a short address.

In the afternoon the Battn. moves at short notice from VAUDRICOURT to HESDIGNEUL.

Casualties this day – NIL.

Maj. E. H. Norman Royal West Kent Regiment takes over Command of the Battalion from this date.

Monday. October 4th. 1915 @ HESDIGNEUL.

Battalion refitting. Battalion Training and Inspections carried out. Nothing eventful occurred during the day.
Casualties this day. – NIL.

Tuesday. October 5th. 1915. @ HESDIGNEUL.

Battalion refitting. Battalion Training, Company Inspections &c., during the day. No Change.

Casualties this day. – NIL.

Wednesday October 6th. 1915 @
HESDIGNEUL and HOUCHIN.

Battalion refitting and training.
No change in events with exception of
orders received to move in the
afternoon to HOUCHIN. Major
J. E. Bano. and Regtl Sergt Major
J. G. Walker granted leave this day,
two hours notice only given but they
managed to catch the train. Battalion
leave HESDIGNEUL at 4pm and
arrive at HOUCHIN @ 5pm and
take up billets. All correct @ 6.30pm.

Casualties this day. NIL.

Thursday. October 7th 1915 @ HOUCHIN.

Battalion refitting and training.
Nothing eventful occurred during the
day. Priests JaRoo and Anfains join Batt.
Casualties NIL.

Friday. October 8th 1915 @ HOUCHIN.

No Change. Casualties NIL
2nd Lieut H. Hants goes to hospital sick.

Saturday October 9th 1915 @ HOUCHIN

Brigade Route March Carried out.
Nothing of event happened during
the day. Battalion still refitting
Casualties - NIL.

Sunday. October 10th 1915. @ HOUCHIN.

No Change. Voluntary services
+ Communion Service for all
denominations during the day.
Nothing eventful occurred.
Casualties – NIL –

Monday. October 11th 1915 – @ HOUCHIN.

German Counter attack @ LOOS and
HULLUCH. Brigade put under
2 hours notice to move if required.
Germans heavily repulsed.
Casualties this day – NIL –

Tuesday. October 12th 1915 @ HOUCHIN.
and MAZINGARBE

Batts still under 2 hours notice.
This notice cancelled and orders received
to move in afternoon to MAZINGARBE.
Batt. Leaves HOUCHIN @ 6pm
marches via NOUEX-LES-MINES
and arrive at MAZINGARBE about
8.30pm. Some little difficulty
caused through insufficient billets
but we made good and eventually
got settled down about 10pm.
Capt Dormer & Lieut Pryce Knight to hospital sick.
Casualties this day – NIL

Wednesday. October 13th 1915 @ MAZINGARBE

Battalion in Reserve for the operations of 1st Division. Operations around HULLUCH successfully carried out. Battalion ready to go up in support at a minutes notice.
Batts stay night @ MAZINGARBE ready at the same time for an instant move.

Casualties this day — NIL —

Thursday. October 14th 1915 @ MAZINGARBE and LOOS.

Battalion in reserve for 1st Division. Order received to take over position occupied by LOYAL NORTH LANCS REGT. Batts left MAZIN GARBE about 5.30pm and march via PHILOSOPHE — LOOS to trenches N. of Chalk Pit. LOOS. Relief completed by midnight. Batts H.Q. in dug out in POSEN ALLEY.

Casualties this day. TWO WOUNDED.
7442. Sgt. Baker Geo. Loyal Ann
1939 Pte Bullen A. Northamptons

Friday. October 15th 1915 @ LOOS.

Battn in front line. A & C Coys in firing line. B & D Coys in support. Occasional shelling. Very quiet otherwise.
Casualties. Two. O. Ranks. wounded
Reinforcement of 90. N.C.Os and men who had arrived previous day reported and joined Battn in the trenches.

Saturday. October 16th 1915. @ LOOS.

Battalion in front line. No change of Coys in the Support. Occasional shelling otherwise fairly quiet.
Casualties this day Other Ranks:-
Two killed Two wounded.

Sunday October 17th 1915 @ LOOS.

Battalion in front line. No change of Coys in firing line and Supports. Occasional shelling otherwise very quiet. Casualties this day as follows. Two other Ranks wounded:-
No. 1616. Sgt. Robin. Wound of leg, hands & face by Shell.
No. 279 Rfn. Steinberg. D. Wound of right forearm by Shell.

Monday. October 18th 1915 @ LOOS.

Battalion in Brigade Reserve in old German Second line. Very quiet all day. Working parties supplied.
Casualties. One other Rank wounded ie L/Cpl. Fisted wound through Carelessly handling rifle

Tuesday October 19th. 1915 @ LOOS.

Battalion in Brigade Reserve in old German Second line trenches. Very quiet all day. Periodical bombardments carried out by our Artillery. (47th Divn Arty.) Casualties this day. One other Rank wounded while on duty with working party.
No. 1534. Bgh. Petit. G. Shot through Stomach.

Battalion relieved in front line by 19th Battalion. Withdrew to field its Reserve in old German Second line near Fosse BLATZ.

Wednesday. October 20th 1915 @ LOOS.

Battalion in Brigade Reserve in old German Second line trenches. Very quiet all day. Periodical Bombardments by our Artillery (47th Divn Arty) Working parties supplied.
Casualties this day — Nil.

Thursday. October. 21st 1915 @ LOOS.

Battalion in Reserve to Brigade in Old German Landline & such till 6pm. At 6.30pm Battalion relieve 18th Batt in front line near FORT. TOSH. Batt. H.Q. at FORT. TOSH. Relief Complete about 9pm. Very quiet this night.

Casualties NIL

Friday. October. 22nd. 1915 @ LOOS.

Battalion in front line near FORT TOSH. Considerable shelling by enemy of our front line & support take place. One Company in front line, 2 Companies in support. 1 Company in Reserve. Casualties as follows ONE other rank.

A/Cpl. 4228. Rfn. King. W.S. wound by Shell of head.

Saturday. October. 23rd 1915 @ LOOS.

Battalion in front line near FORT TOSH. One Coy in front line — 2 Coys in Support, 1 Coy in Reserve. 20th & 1st Regt. on our left and French Brigade on our right. Enemy Shell front line & Support very heavily. Trenches enfiladed with shell fire.

Casualties

A.Co.	2379.	A/Cpl. Howell. S.		Shock.
"	1894	Rfn. Redpath. S.H.		—do—
"	1915	" Warren. G.		—do—
"	1279	Cpl. Whale. A.	Dying to be dumb.	
"	3111	L/Cpl. Pearce. Jnr.		Shock.
"	2072	A/Cpl. Smith. B.		—do— Shell of scarf
"	1395	Rfn. Wrightman. G.		—do—
"	3195	" Coggin. F.		—do—
"	1511	" Robins. L.		—do—
"	3113	" Wickham. W.T.		—do—
"	1318	" Foster. J.		Shell of face
"	2085	Sgt. Rothen. S.		Shock.

Sunday. October 24th 1915 @ LOOS.

Battalion in front line near FORT TOSH
1 Coy in front line, 2 Coys in Support,
1 Coy in Reserve. Battn H.Q. FORT TOSH.
Enemy Shell front line Supports
very heavily during the day.
Own Artillery retaliated mainly
Periodical Bombardments carried
out by Field & Heavy Artillery
(4)th Div Division.)
Battn H.Q. Shelled with Light
H.V. Shells. No damage resulting.
Casualties this day:-
One other Ranks wounded.
No. 2355. Rfm. Wilson J. Ebay. Sight head
wound from Shell Splinter.

Monday. October 25th. 1915 @ LOOS.

Battalion in front line near FORT TOSH
1 Coy in firing line, 2 Coys in
Support. 1 Coy in Reserve.
Battn H.Q. at FORT TOSH.
Trenches under enfilade fire
from enemy. Enemy Shell
front line & Supports very
heavily. Periodical bombardments
retaliation carried out by our
Artillery. (4) Div Arty).
Enemy Shell Battn H.Q. with
L.H.V. Shells. No damage resulting
Casualties this day:-
One other Ranks wounded.
No. 3521. Rfm. Owens E. wound of Shoulder
Ebay. by Shell.

Casualty caused through Carelessness.
Self Inflicted. No. 4619. Rfm Devall. H.
A Coy. Wound of left foot by
bullet while cleaning his rifle.

Tuesday. October. 26th. 1915 @ LOOS.

Battalion in front line near Fort 70 St.
1 Coy firing line, 2 Coys in support
1 Coy in reserve. This day the
enemy shelled our trenches
very heavily causing several
casualties. During the shelling
of the trenches a man Rfn Peat
was buried, just leaving his head out
of the earth and free to the open air
several went to his rescue and
in so doing either lost their lives
or were severely wounded.
Lieut. Robert Louis Carpenter & 2nd Lieut
John Alexander Ross of D Coy
were killed outright when attempting
rescue took also several riflemen
Captain Hector McKay Calder
tendered valuable work by
attending to the bants of Rifle
wounded men under heavy
shell fire. Casualties for this
day were as follows.

2 Officers killed

Lieut. Robert Louis Carpenter
2nd Lieut John Alexander Ross

Other Ranks killed 9
Missing 2.
Wounded 8. Shock 8.

The missing were Rfn
Devanney and Rfn Menok
of D Coy. They both went
to the rescue of their comrades
and in so doing lost their
lives. (These men though
buried in the trenches by
shell fire could not be found
although a party were set
off to try and dig them
out. They were eventually
reported as missing

Wednesday October 27th 1915 @ LOOS.

Battalion in front line. 1 Company in firing line. 2 Company's in support, and 1 Company in Reserve trenches. Battn. H.Q. @ FORT TOSH.
Enemy again enfilade our front line and support trenches with shell fire, armour piercing shells causing considerable Casualties, mostly firing line trench. DOUBLE TOWERS LOOS Shelled heavily in the afternoon. Our artillery carried out periodical bombardments in conjunction with the 15th Divisional artillery. On our left the 19th Battalion. On our right the London Regiment. Casualties this day were 2 Killed, and 10 wounded.

2/Lieut. L. G. Smith joined Battalion this day for duty.
2/Lieut. P. A. Starke leaves for hospital with shock.

Thursday October 28th 1915 @ LOOS.

Battalion in front line. 1 Company in firing line. 2 Company in support, and 1 Company in Reserve trenches. Battalion H.Q. at FORT TOSH.
Enemy again shell our front line and support trenches causing several Casualties.
The Battalion on our right the 18th Lon Regt. also had several Casualties during the day. During the tour in the trenches those that were badly wounded had to lay in the trenches until dark, as they were to exposed to the enemy's rifle to evacuate them to be brought down during the day time.
Burial Service of Weight N.C.O's and Men Killed during 26/25 instant. Service Conducted by Rev. C.T.T. Wood. 1st Batt. Blk (Chaplain) first outside H.Q. at Ft. Tosh.
(Casualties during this day 3 Killed, 3 wounded.
2/Lieut. G. J. Fitch returns from sick leave.

Friday. October 29th. 1915 @ LOOS.

Battalion in front line. 1 Company in firing line, 1 Companies in support, and 1 Company in Reserve trenches.
Battalion H.Q. at FORT. TOSH.
Enemy again shell our trenches heavily. Also the Battalion on our left (18th/Lon Regt) and the french on our right. In the afternoon an attack expected by us and stand to to ordered. Nothing happened and orders were eventually sent round to "Stand down". Relief expected tomorrow night the 20th indicant. 140th Bde being relieved by the 140th Bde.
Burial Service this evening conducted by Revd. L.J.V. Wood and Captain R.C. Gunner (22nd/Lon Regt) attestations. Place of burials just outside H.Q. at FORT TOSH.
Casualties this day included Stretcher Wounded. Other Ranks.

Saturday October 30th 1915 @ LOOS and LE PHILOSOPHE.

Battalion in fort line up to 8. O.P.M.
1 Company in firing line, 1 Company in support and 1 Company in Reserve trenches. Enemy shell trenches again early during the day causing casualties as follows
O. Ranks. 1 Killed and 5 Wounded.
Battalion this day relieved by the 8th Bn London Regt (Storr RC.), handed over Battalion trenches took to LE PHILOSOPHE and acts as reserve for the 140th Inf Bde 18th, 19th & 20th Battns go to MAZINGARBE to Divisional Reserve. Battalion march took in platoons at 200 yards interval via LOOS. - BENE/FONTAINE RD - LENS - BETHUNE ROAD to LE PHILOSOPHE. Battalion arrives and take over billets vacated by the 23rd London Regiment at PHILOSOPHE. All correct and in billets by Midnight.
Battalion H.Q. just near old VERMELLES STATION.
2/Lieut. W.E. Borden and 38 other Ranks. Join Battn from Base. Lieut Borden took Commission from Ranks to Sergt in Corp of Hooton.

Sunday. October 31st 1915 @
LE PHILOSOPHE.

Battn in reserve for the 140th Brigade.
Day spent in cleaning up
and bathing. 2/Lieut. G.S. Brice
joined Battalion from Base.
Nothing eventful happened during the
day. Casualties NIL.

Monday. November 1st 1915 @ LE PHILOSOPHE
Battn in reserve for the 140th Brigade.
Bathing &c. carried out during
the day. New draft of 38 which
joined Bttn on the 30th and of 90
which joined us in the trenches @
LOOS (FORT GLATZ) inspected this day
by the Commanding Officer. Periodical
Bombardments by the Batteries located
around PHILOSOPHE — MAZINGARBE, and
VERMELLES. Casualties this day NIL.

Tuesday. 2nd November 2nd. 1915 @
LE PHILOSOPHE.

Battalion in reserve for the 140th Brigade.
Bathing and Company inspections
carried out. Periodical bombardment
of the enemy's line around LOOS - HULLUCH
by our Artillery (47th Div Arty in
conjunction with 15th Div Arty and the
French) Nothing eventful happened
during the day. Casualties NIL.

Wednesday. November 3rd. 1915 @
LE PHILOSOPHE

Battn in reserve for the 140th Brigade
Company Inspections by Coy Commanders
during the day. Small bombardments
carried out by our Artillery.
Nothing of importance happened
during the day.
Casualties this day — NIL.

Saturday November 6th 1915 @ LE PHILOSOPHE
and OLD GERMAN SECOND LINE TRENCH in Coal
Recess.

Battalion in reserve for 140th Inf Bde
up to 6.0 p.m. Lord Mayor of London
inspects our Battalion at PHILOSOPHE
at 12.30 p.m. He had already inspected
the other 3 Battns of our Brigade ie
18th 19th & 20th Battalions at MAZINGARBE.
He was accompanied by General Barter
Commander of the Division (47th London Div) and
Divisional Staff during his tour of
inspection. He was highly satisfied
with the inspection of our Battalion.
He afterwards left PHILOSOPHE to inspect
the other Units of the 140th and 142nd
Inf Bde in the front line between
LOOS and HULLUCH. Battalion
relieves 23rd London Regiment in old German
Second line in B Sector near LONE TREE
and carry out relief via VICTORIA
STATION and BSEN STATION. Relief
completed about 11 p.m. Battn H.Q.
in trenches. Casualties this day. Nil.

Thursday November 4th 1915 @ LE PHILOSOPHE

Battalion in reserve for the 140th Bde.
Company inspections by the Company
Commanders during the day
Battn. and inspection of Rifles
by the Commanding Officer. Periodical
Bombardments on the enemy front by
our Artillery. Nothing of Importance
to relate this day.
Casualties this day — NIL

Friday November 5th 1915 @ LE PHILOSOPHE

Battalion in reserve for the 140th Bde
Company inspections by Company Commanders
Rifle inspection also carried out. Usual
Periodical bombardments by our
Artillery located round PHILOSOPHE
VERMELLES and MAZINGARBE.
Nothing of Importance to relate. Information
received that our Brigade is to relieve 142 Bde
tomorrow night in B Sector between LOOS and
HULLUCH. Casualties this day NIL.

Wednesday November 10th 1915 @ LOOS. (B.Sect.)

Battalion in reserve trenches and in
Local reserve for our Brigade (What Suffolks)
until 5. O.pm. Batt. relieve 5th
Batt. for Regt. in firing line.
All complete no regards relief by
10. O. pm. Rations during this
period of front line duty in the trenches
were brought up in trucks on wooden
railroad constructed by R.E.'s from
Victoria Station on the VERMELLES
Road to POSEN STATION near the
reserve trenches. They were then
collected by fatigue parties of the
Batt. Periodical Bombardments
of the German front line during
the day and night by our
artillery. Enemy retaliated with
small shells on our trenches, but
caused no damage. Trenches in
very bad condition owing to the excessive
amount of rain, and in places up
to one's knees in water.
Casualties during the day — NIL.

Sunday November 7th 1915 @ LOOS. (front
line). B. Section in reserve in (OLD) GERMAN 2nd LINE.

Battalion in reserve trenches and in local
reserve for What-Bde. Very quiet during
the day. Periodical Bombardments
by our artillery, otherwise nothing
of importance learned. Casualties
this day. One other rank killed by
falling in of dug out.
2/Lieut. W.D. Bates became suddenly ill
and was sent to hospital.

Monday November 8th 1915 @ LOOS. (B.Sect)

Battalion in reserve trenches in B.Sect.
Reserve for our own Brigade.
Nothing of importance to relate.
Casualties. NIL.
2/Lieut. G.W. Bird to hospital this
day sick.

November 9th 1915 @ LOOS. (B.Sect.)

No Change. Casualties NIL.
in reserve.

Thursday. November 11th 1915 @ LOOS (B. Scots)
front line.

3 Companies in front line. 1 Company in support. Battn H.Q. in support trenches. Periodical Bombardment by our Artillery. Germans retaliate with L.H.V. Shells on support trenches and around H.Q. No damage resulting. Otherwise than above it was very quiet during the day.

Casualties during the day NIL —

Friday. November 12th 1915 @ LOOS (B. Scots)
Front line

A, B & C Companies in firing line. D Company in support. Battn H.Q. in support trenches in dug out. Very quiet all day, with the exception of a few L.H.V. Shells around H.Q. and support trenches.

Casualties this day. NIL

Saturday. November 13th 1915 @ LOOS
(B. Scots) Front line and LE PHILOSOPHE

Battn in front line till 6.0 p.m.
B, C & D Companies in firing line. A Coy in support. Battn H.Q. situated in support trenches. Very quiet all day. Battn relieved by the 2nd K.R.R's about 6.0 p.m. and march back into billets in reserve via POSEN STATION along railway line (vide map) cordinates trk. E.4 to VICTORIA STATION thence down VERMELLES-LENS Road to PHILOSOPHE by platoons at 200 yards interval. Relief Completed and all in billets about midnight. 4/4th (Lon) Division to be relieved by 1st Dn and to fall back into Corps Reserve for H.Q. works.

Casualties this day — NIL

18th, 19th and 20th Battalions with Brigade H.Q. goe to MAZINGARBE to Rest for the night.

Sunday. November. 12th LE PHILOSOPHE. and
LILLE.R.S.

Battalion leaves PHILOSOPHE and entrains
with 18th 19th and 20th Battalions for
LILLERS, marching via MAZINGARBE to
NOEUX-LES-MINES Station. Battalion
arrive at LILLERS about H.O.hm. where
they take up billets and rest for
one night before proceeding to place
allotted during the period they are at
rest not in Corps Reserve.
Casualties during the day – NIL.
Transport Marched from MAZINGARBE to LILLERS.

Monday. November 15th 1915 @ LILLERS and
BURBURE.

Battalion leaves LILLERS where they had been
resting for the night and March to BURBURE
their place of rest during the period
they are in Corps Reserve for the 4th
Corps. Leave LILLERS about 11am
and arrive BURBURE about mid-day.

Billets taken over but we were informed
that they were in our wrong area and
therefore had to move to the other billets
at the other end of the village.
Battn. eventually get into billets about
H.O.hm. The other Battalions of
the Brigade (18th 19th and 20th Yorks Regt)
and Brigade H.Q. take over billets
at PARISBERT. Battn. H.Q.
situated on the BURBURE-RAMBERT
ROAD.
Casualties this day – NIL.

Tuesday. November. 16th 1915 @ BURBURE.

Battalion in Corps Reserve for 4th Corps and
under 2 hour notice to move in the event
of any emergency. Battalion
cleaning up after trench work during
the day. Nothing of importance
to relate.
Casualties this day NIL.

Wednesday November 17th 1915 @ BURBURE

Battalion in Corps Reserve for 4th Corps.
Refitting of Battalion and Company
Inspections carried out this day.
C.O. inspects billets.

Casualties this day NIL

Thursday November 18th 1915 @ BURBURE

Battalion in Corps Reserve for 4th Corps.
Refitting of Battalion. Cleaning up.
Company inspections carried out.
Commanding Officers drew up
programme of Officers training, and
Battn School of Instruction for Recruits,
Young Officers, N.C.Os and prospective
N.C.Os arranged.
Advised from Brigade that 2 Officers and
106 N.C.Os and men arrive next day
as reinforcement for the Battn.

Casualties this day — NIL

Friday November 19th 1915 @ BURBURE

Battalion in Corps Reserve for 4th Corps.
First day of training as per programme
held. 2 Officers and 106 N.C.Os
and Men arrive from Base as
reinforcement. Officers:- 2nd Lieut.
A.E. Stubbs and 2nd Lieut. A.H. McCracken.
New arrivals posted to Companies.

Casualties this day NIL

Saturday November 20th 1915 @ BURBURE

Battalion in Corps Reserve for 4th Corps.
Classes of Instruction for Young Officers,
N.C.Os & Recruits under Battn arrangement
this day. Another new officer
arrives from Base viz. 2nd Lieut.
C.J. Booth.

Casualties this day Nil

Sunday November 21st. 1915 @ BURBURE

Batt. in Corps Reserve for H/qrs.
Divine Service: Church of England
Nonconformist, Catholics & Church this
day. Training carried out
today.
Lieutenant & Quartermaster
J. J. Townsend leaves Battalion for
hospital. This officer had been
in very bad health for some time
passed.
Commander of 14th Inf. Bde. inspects transport lines
Casualties this day NIL.

———

Monday. November 22nd. 1915 @ BURBURE

Battalion in Corps Reserve for H/qrs.
G.O.C. 14th Bde. inspects Transport of
the Battalion. 2/Lt. Fr. Croft took over
command of Grenadier Platoon vice 2/Lt. G.A.
Clarke returned for duty and posted
to B. Company. B.Q. Recreation Room

joined at RAIMBERT on the AUCHEL
road.
Casualties this day – NIL.

———

Tuesday November 23rd at BURBURE
Bath in Corps Reserve for H/Qrs.
G.O.C. 14th Brigade inspected last
draft and young officers on the recruits
training ground. Casualties Nil.
Bkfst firing on Range at U 29 a

———

Wednesday November 24th 1915 at BURBURE
Battn in Corps Reserve for H/Qrs
"B" Company fires on Range at U.29.a.
"A" and "C" Coy attended demonstrations
in Field Engineering at Bde R.E. School
Series of Classes in French Cooking
Under Sergt Mackerlock (Sergt Major) commences
attended by one man per platoon.
2/Lt. H. Edwards appointed to command
Lewis Machine Gun Section, with
section of 3 N.C.Os + 24 Riflemen
Casualties this day - Nil

Thursday November 25th 1915 at BURBURE

Battalion in Corps Reserve to 4th Corps
Morning. Battalion Route March —
Route — BURBURE - C.12 - VOLINGHEM
— AUCHEL - RAHMBERT - BURBURE.
"Bay Jones" Adv. Guard.
Afternoon. Bands "D" Coy attended
demonstration in Field Engineering
at Bae R.E. School.
Casualties this day — NIL.

2nd Bn Bomb Course commenced.
2/Lt E.J. Booth + 12 OR detailed to attend.
Casualties this day — NIL.

Saturday November 27th 1915 at BURBURE
Bn in Corps Reserve to 4th Corps
Fatigue party of 25 men under a
Sergeant sent to Officer i/c Flying Ground
at HESDIGNEUL.
Casualties this day — NIL

Sunday November 28th 1915 at BURBURE
Battalion in Corps Reserve to 4th
Corps.
Divine Service for all denominations
during the day.
2/Lt E.G. Smith and 11 OR to Div
Bomb School. 3 OR to I.M. School.
12 OR from I.M.G. Section to Maxim
Course at Bae. 2/Lt A.A. McCracken
and 10 OR to L.M.G. School.
Casualties this day — NIL

Friday November 26th 1915 at BURBURE
Bn in Corps Reserve to 4th Corps
Bathing arranged for Bn from 9am
to 12:15 pm. Billets inspected at 10 am
by A.D.M.S. Lecture by Brigadier to all
Officers at Recreation Room RAHMBERT.
Lieut & Q.M. Gyfformers Evacuated to
ENGLAND. Gas Demonstration at Bae
Bombing School. Trenches at 2:15 pm - attended
by 50 rank from each of A B + C Coys. 2/Lt D. Forbes
2/Lt E.G. Smith 2/Lt A.L. Shorter, 2/Lt A.A. McCracken
+ 2/Lt R.R. O'Brien
the whole party under Capt R.R. O'Brien

Monday November 29th 1915 at BURBURE.

Battalion in Corps Reserve
to 4th Corps.
Bn route march arranged but
cancelled on notification from Bde
that Divisional Route march had
been arranged for following day
Casualties this day — NIL.

Tuesday November 30th 1915 at BURBURE
Bn in Corps Reserve to 4th Corps.
Div. Route March postponed
Companies at disposal of Company
Commanders
Casualties this day — NIL.

Wednesday December 1st 1915 at BURBURE.
Bn in Corps Reserve to 4th Corps.
Divisional Route March & Exercise
commenced. 17th Bn paraded on
LILLERS road at U.27.a.7.1.

Scheme — Enemy reported on the line
POPERINGHE — CASSEL — WATTEN in touch
with our Cavalry who are covering the
front of the Army.
First Div. on right and 15th Div on
left of 47th Div.
47th Div advanced in direction of
ST. OMER — route via ST. HILAIRE —
LAMBRES road junction to mile W. of AIRE —
RINCQ — QUESTEDE.

Objects of Exercise:
(a) To give Staffs and Units an opportunity
of practicing:—
(a) The writing and rapid issue of orders.
(b) The rapid billeting of troops from the
line of March
(c) Starting troops on the march from billets
without unnecessary delay and hardship
to the troops
(d) March discipline.
(e) The service of protection on the
march and in billets
(f) Packing of transport vehicles and care
of animals on the march.

(9)

(9) Supply arrangements for troops on the march.
47th Div billeted for the night in the area LIETTRES - QUERNES - WITTERNESSE - ST. QUENTIN - RINCQ - WARNE - ROQUETOIRE - REBECQ - CRECQUES - MARTHES - BLESSY.

Casualties this day - NIL.

Thursday December 2nd.915 - ON TREK.

Bn in Corps Reserve to 4th Corps. Return journey from Rx Route march & exercise. Bn arriving at BURBURE about 3pm.
Total number who fell out on the march - Officers nil. OR 36.

Casualties this day - NIL.

Friday December 3rd.915 at BURBURE
Bn in Corps Reserve to 4th Corps. Companies at disposal of Company Commanders. 2lb a.6 Stubbs and 3

trained Signallers to Div Signalling Course.

Casualties this day - NIL.

Saturday December 4th.915 at BURBURE.
Battalion in Corps Reserve to 4th Corps. Recruits parade for Musketry on range

Casualties for this day - NIL.

Sunday December 5th.915 at BURBURE
Bn in Corps Reserve to 4th Corps. Divine Service for all denominations. Special Service in Theatre LILLERS by Rev M. Adler for Jewish Soldiers.

L.m.G. Section attaches for pay rations + administration to 16th Coy. #/L.C. I Booth + 11 OR to Div Bomb School. 3 OR to I.M. School L.W.A. Clarke and 10 OR to Div L.M.G. School.

Casualties this day - NIL.

Monday 6th December 1915 at BURBURE
Bn in Corps Reserve to 4th Corps
A.B & C Coys instructed in Bombing at
Grenadier Training Grounds. M. Flak appt. Adjt
Lecture by Brigadier to Coys, 2nd in
command and Coy Commanders of all Bns & all offrs
and Coy Commanders of all Bn & Sertfs
Casualties this day – NIL

Tuesday 7th December 1915 at BURBURE.
Tactical exercise for all C.Os, 2nds in
command & Coy Commanders of all Bns
of Bde.
Casualties this day – NIL

Wednesday 8th December 1915 at BURBURE
Bn in Corps Reserve to 4th Corps
A & B Coys route march under Majors
K.N O'Brien. C & D Coys 13/4 hours each
Bombing under instruction of Lts.
J.H. Wright (Grenadier Officer)
Casualties this day NIL
Social Evening at Recreation Room
RAIMBERT, conducted by Rev J Blackbourne

Senior Chaplain 1st Army. Lantern
Slides & Choruses.
Major L Evans Evans to Hospital.

Thursday December 9th 1915 at BURBURE
Bn in Corps Reserve to 4th Corps
Bathing from 10am to 4pm for whole
Bn. C & A Coys Grenadiers
2/Lieut C.G. Smith + 6 N.C.Os for
Bde Field Engineering Course.
Capt K.N O'Brien and 2 NCOs + 12
Ops attended Bde Wiring Course (3 days)
Course.

Bde Grenade Competition, Individual
and Knockout Events. L/Cpl Schwabe
of this Bn won third place in Individual
Competition was selected as one of
Bde representatives for Divisional Competition
10-12-15.
Casualties this day. NIL

Friday, December 10th 1915 at BURBURE

Bn in Corps Reserve to 4th Corps
Companies at disposal of Coy
Commanders.
Bathing for A Coy Grenadiers
commencing at 10 a.m.
Commanding Officer & Coy Comdrs
reconnoitre "C" Sector - to be at H.Q.
at NOEULLES at 7 a.m.
Capt K.R. O'Brien to Hospital
Casualties this day NIL

Saturday December 11th 1915 at BURBURE

Bn in Corps Reserve to 4th Corps.
Bn Route March - BURBURE -
HURIONVILLE - ECQUEDECQUES - BOURECQ -
LILLERS - BURBURE.
Casualties this day :- NIL

Sunday, December 12th 1915 at BURBURE

Bn in Corps Reserve to 4th Corps
Divine Service for all denominations,
including Special Service at LILLERS
for Jewish Soldiers.
2/Lt K.J. Stokes and 11 O.R.'s
Div Bomb School. 2/Lt C.J. Booth
and 3 O.R. to Div L.M.G. School
2/Lt H. of Carter returnes from
hospital.
Final of Inter-platoon Football
Competition - 13 platoon beat 8 platoon
by 4-1.
Billetting party proceed to SAILLY -
LABOURSE.
Casualties this day - NIL

Monday December 13th 1915 at BURBURE & SAILLY LABOURSE

1/4 of Bn relieved 2th Inf Bde.
1/4 Bn entrained at LILLERS at 9 a.m.
and proceed by train to NOEUX, marching
from NOEUX to SAILLY LABOURSE, and taking

over billets of 8th K.O.S.B.
Bn HQ established at junction
ANNEQUIN – LABOURSE roads.
Casualties this day – Nil.

Tuesday December 14th/1915 at SAILLY LABOURSE

14/1st Bde relieves 44th Bde in
K. sector. 17th Bn relieves 8th
SEAFORTHS in C.1, being met by guides
of that Bn at WATER TOWER at entrance
of CHAPEL ALLEY at 7.30 a.m.
M. Guns of 17th Bn relieves M.
Guns of 8th Seaforths in C.1.
Combined Orderly Room system
inaugurated. O.R. Clerks of H.Bns accommodated
in Combined Orderly Room in NOYELLES
opposite church.
Quiet day – Casualties NIL.

Wednesday December 15th 1915 at VERMELLES

Bn in Front Line of C.1.
Slight shelling by enemy but no

damage. Casualties this day – Nil.
Draft of 35 ORs arrived from Base.
Major J. Evan Evans evacuated to
England. 7th M. Lors Hospital

Thursday December 16th 1915 at VERMELLES.

Disposition of Bn unchanged.
Quiet day, some shelling.
Casualties this day – 5 ORs wounded.

Friday December 17th 1915 at NOYELLES.

Bn relieved in C.1. sector by 20th
Som Regt, and proceeded into Bde Reserve
at NOYELLES
Casualties this day – Nil

Saturday December 18th 1915 at NOYELLES.

Bn in Brigade Reserve.
Working party of 75 of A Coy + 75 of
B Coy, with 7 SCOs extra, under Captain
V.C. Bowden, 2/Lt E.G. Smith, 2/Lt A.B. Kitts
P.T.O.

to report to 3rd Lon R.F. at VERMELLES Church at 6.30pm for carrying Trench Gratings – making 2 journeys. This party reported back at Bn H.Q. at 11.30pm

C & D Coys each provided party of 25 men under 2/Lt A.H. McBracken, to report to 3rd Lon R.F. at VERMELLES Church at 6.45pm to carry pickets and sandbags – making 2 journeys.
Casualties this day – NIL

Sunday December 19th 1915 – at NOYELLES and VAUDRICOURT

14/Lon Bde relieved by 140th Bde 1/7th Bn relieves by 1st Bn London Regt and proceeded to VAUDRICOURT via SAILLY-LABOURSE – LABOURSE – VERQUIGNEUL – VERQUIN.

Number of men who fell out on march – 3
Casualties this day – NIL

Monday December 20th 1915 at VAUDRICOURT

Brigade in Divisional Reserve
Companies at disposal of Company Commanders.
2/Lt G.D. Gibb Jones Bn from Base
Casualties this day – NIL

Tuesday December 21st 1915 at VAUDRICOURT

Brigade in Divisional Reserve
Companies inspected by B.O. Companies inspected by C.O. as under:–

A Co 10/30am   B Co 11am   C.C 11:30 am
D Co noon   M.G. Section 12:30pm

Draft of 35 O.R. who joined Bn on 15th inst at NOYELLES proceeded to Bde HQ at LABOURSE under 2/Lt A.H. Gibb for inspection by G.O.C. 141st L. Bde.
2/Lt A.J. Parke proceeded to Bn Bomb School as instructor. 2/Lt M. Murray for 7 days course.

Casualties this day – NIL

Wednesday, December 22nd/15 @ VAUDRICOURT

Brigade in Divisional Reserve.
Companies at disposal of
Company Commanders
Casualties day – NIL

Thursday December 23rd/15 @ SAILLY LABOURSE
and in D Sector

1st Bn relieves 1/42nd Bde in
D Sector.
Combined Orderly Room established
in SAILLY LABOURSE at junction
MINE QUIN – LABOURSE roads.
Bn relieves 21st & 22nd Bns in
D1. Section – Bn H Qrs at G.11.a.0.8,
marching direct from VAUDRICOURT
5.30 a.m.
2/Lt A.W. Cracken + 36 O.R. places
at disposal of C.R.E. as permanent
working party during period Bn is held
D Sector.
Quiet day. Enemy flung their rifle grenades

about junction of saps but did no
damage.
Casualties this day – NIL

Friday December 24th/15 at SAILLY-LABOURSE
and in D Sector

R.E. exploded mine near G.11.6.12.35,
after which our artillery kept up heavy
bombardment on the Germans front and
support trenches. 18th Bn had heavy
casualties in connection with this
mining operation.
9 officers + 15 O.R. of 6th Connaught
Rangers attached for instruction from
24th to 26th incl.
Casualties of considerable dimensions
at junction of ALEXANDER TRENCH –
RIFLEMAN ALLEY – CROWN TRENCH.
Repaired next day by fatg of D/1 Bn
Quiet on our front – Casualties NIL

Saturday December 25th/9/15 at SAILLY LABOURSE and VERMELLES

Battalion relieved by 20th Bn and moved into support with one Company in LANCASHIRE TRENCH, one Coy in VERMELLES, one Coy in Railway Reserve Trench and one Company garrison for KEEPS by day & sleeping in VERMELLES at nights.
3 carrying parties of one Officer and 50 men for carrying trench gratings under 3rd Bde R.E.
1/L.Y.R. Gift and 11 O.R. proceeded to Div Bomb School. 5 O.R. to Div LMG School.
Armstrong Shelt for Farmer drawn from 3rd Bde R.E.
Casualties this day – NIL

Sunday December 26th/9/15 at SAILLY-LABOURSE and VERMELLES

Battalion in Support – Disposition as yesterday.
Mine exploded by enemy. Lewis Machine Gun slightly damaged by Shrapnel. M.G. Stark to hospital.
Quiet day – Casualties NIL

Monday December 27th/9/15 at SAILLY-LABOURSE and VERMELLES

"A" Coy took over from left front Coy in D.1.
"B" Coy took over from right front Coy in D.1.
One T.M. Barraged NEW CRATER at KINK
2 TMs barraged craters in front of Sap 7.
Mine exploded by enemy.
Fairly quiet day – Casualties NIL

Tuesday December 28th 1915 at SAILLY LABOURSE and VERMELLES.

Disposition of Bn as yesterday. Enemy shelled with heavy shells but did no damage.
Casualties this day – Nil.

Wednesday December 29th/15 at SAILLY-LABOURSE and VERMELLES.

Disposition of Bn as yesterday. Artillery bombardment of German system at G.5.a.6.2.1 between 3pm & 3.30pm with 18 pounders and heavy Howitzers. During bombardment disposition of Bn altered as under:- Front face of Craters/French evacuated. B Coy N & E of Crate moves to ALEXANDER TRENCH, S. of GRENADIER TRENCH. B Coy S & W of CRATER moves to CROWN TRENCH and GRENADIER LOOP S of GRENADIER TRENCH. Two platoons of C Coy in CROWNTRENCH moves into N.E. end of HULLUCH ALLEY. Right platoon of A Coy moves into GORDON ALLEY forming support platoon in TS in this trench.

Enemy firing rifle grenades at left front Coy in the evening – Artillery retaliates.
2/Lt S. Owen joined infantry school from Base – also draft of 9 men. This draft should have been 20 men but one got lost and joined Bn direct.
Casualties this day – Nil.

Thursday December 30th/15 at SAILLY-LABOURSE

Battalion relieves in D.1. by 2/4th York Regt and moves into Bde Reserve at SAILLY LABOURSE.
Casualties this day – Nil.

Friday December 31st 1915 at VERQUIN

1st/4th Bn. on relief by 14th/
Bde. moved into Divisional Reserve.
17th Bn. marched via SAILLY LABOURSE —
LABOURSE — VERQUIN — establishing
Bn.H.Q. at VERQUIN CHATEAU, at about
12.30 p.m. 2/Lt. J. Hollum remained
in billets at SAILLY LABOURSE for 3 hours
after Battalion left to cope any claims.
Bn. at 2 hours notice whilst
in Bn. Reserve
Casualties — Nil.

Saturday January 1st 1916. at VERQUIN.

Bn. in Div. Reserve.
2nd Lt. J.L. Barter appointed acting Adjutant.
2/Lt. W.H. McCracken attached to 14th Bde. M.G. Coy.
Vice 2/Lt. J.L. Barter.
Casualties — Nil.

Sunday January 2nd 1916 at VERQUIN.

Officers reconnoitred Loos Sector, N. Subsection
prior to Bn. taking over.
Casualties — Nil

Monday January 3rd 1916 at VERQUIN & LE BREBIS.

Bn. left VERQUIN at 11.a.m. and marched to
LE BREBIS which place was being shelled on arrival.
Four of billeting party wounded by Shell, 3 remaining
at duty, and one (Capt. J. Alcock) being evacuated
subsequently being transferred to England

Tuesday January 4th 1916. at N.&S. BREBIS & Loos.

Bn. moved at 4.30 p.m. from LE BREBIS and
took over N. Sub Section Loos Sector. Bn. H.Q. at
Cité St. LAURENT. Left maps:–
G.36.a. + 9.3. Limits of Subsection Loos. Cité St. LAURENT. Sheet N°3.
exclusive to H.31.c.6.9. Relief completed about 10 p.m.   Open Sqrs. 3
Casualties — Nil.

Wednesday 5th January 1916. at Loos N sub sector.

Telephonic communication established with Liaison Officer of BAUDIT Group, French Arty. Support line heavily shelled between 10.50 am at 11.30 am. — Otherwise quiet day.
Casualties – 3 O.R. wounded by shell fire.

Thursday 6th January 1916. Loos N. Sub Sector.

Enemy artillery active with L.H.V. (also T.M.) more especially against right front Company. Bn. relieved by 9th Bn. 2nd and moved into support with two companies in LOOS and two companies in N. MAROC. Bn. H.Q. in N. MAROC. Quiet day. Casualties — nil.

Friday
~~Wednesday~~ 7th January 1916. at Loos N. Sub Sector & N. MAROC.

Bttn. in support. Disposition unchanged. LOOS shelled with 8 heavies.
Casualties – 4 O.R. killed, 9 O.R. wounded. Casualties caused by shell entering cellar and bursting inside.

Saturday 8th January 1916. at Loos.

Relieved 8th. Bn. in Centre subsector. Loos Sector Subsection limits – Loos – PAGE 12 Av incl to Loos – Ref map C. 14 St LAURENT Rd. inclusive. Bn. H.Q. at G.b.c.88. 36.C.N.3. Fair 3.
Casualties – nil.

Sunday 9th January 1916. at Loos Centre subsector.

Enemy artillery active during day. Carrying party seen by enemy and communication trench shelled (10.20 am) worth delayed till dusk. Casualties – nil.

Monday 10th January 1916. at Loos Centre subsector.

Enemy artillery busy all day with guns of all calibre. Our artillery retaliated with Heavies on German barrier on Loos-HULLUCH Rd.
Casualties – nil.

Tuesday 11th January 1916. at LOOS. centre subsection.

Enemy snipers active during early morning. Enemy shelled CHALK PIT with heavies and CRASSIER with shrapnel. Casualties:- 2nd Lt. J.T. FORBES severely wounded by sniper bullet in head.

Wednesday 12th January 1916. LOOS. Centre subsection.

Enemy fired rifle grenades and occasional bombs of H.E. on CRASSIER. Bn. relieved by 6th Bn. and moved back into LES BREBIS. Casualties:- Sgt. A.H. Jackson killed by rifle grenade.

Thursday 13th January 1916. at LES BREBIS.

Bn. in Biv. Reserve. Quiet day. Casualties – Nil.

Friday 14th January 1916 at LES BREBIS.

Bn. in Biv. Reserve. Quiet day. Casualties – Nil.

Saturday. 15th. Jan. 1916. at LES BREBIS.

Bn. in Biv. Reserve. Quiet day. Working Party of 3 Officers and 100 O.R. supplied for work under R.E. on road from FOSSE 2 to LES BREBIS from 9am. to 12 noon. Casualties – Nil.
1 Officer and 50 OR. for work under R.E. from 9am to 12 noon. Casualties – Nil.

Sunday 16th. Jan. 1916. at LES BREBIS. & MAROC.

Bn. took over right subsection MAROC sector from 22nd Bn. & Platoon 7th LEINSTER Regt. attached. Relief complete about 8.50 pm. Disposition:-
Right Front – D. Coy. and 1 platoon LEINSTERS.
Left Front – B. Coy. and 1 platoon LEINSTERS. Support – C. Coy. and 2 platoons LEINSTERS. Reserve – A. Coy.
Casualties – 1 killed by sniper during relief.
3 men decorated with T.C.M. ribbons by G.O.C. 47 Divn.

Monday, 17th. Jan. 1916. at MAROC.

Disposition unchanged. Quiet day. Carrying parties for rations and R.E. stores provided by 7th LEINSTERS. 2nd Lt. FORBES (wounded 11/1/16) died in hospital at LILLERS, buried at LILLERS cemetery. Casualties – Nil.

Sunday. 18th Jan. 1916. at MAROC Sector RIGHT Subsector.

Disposition unchanged. Quiet day. Patrol reported large enemy working party from N.9.E.9.1.10 Ry map N.9.C.4.4. fired on by Machine Guns. also Covering party on SUNKEN Rd. Artillery fired Rg. map 3gc N.M.3 Fair. 3 but concentration of one round per gun by all guns on the front at 3pm. Casualties - Nil.

Wednesday. 19th Jan. 1916. at MAROC Sector RIGHT Subsector.

Dispositions unchanged. Quiet day. Two enemy working parties about 100 strong in front of PUIT 16 and PUIT 11 bis dispersed by Artillery. Casualties.

Thursday. 20th Jan. 1916. at MAROC Sector RIGHT Subsector.

Dispositions unchanged. Quiet day. Casualties - Nil.

Friday. 21st Jan. 1916. at MAROC Sector RIGHT Subsector.

Disposition Sun changed. L.M.G's of 7th. LEINSTERS attached for instruction. Our artillery bombarded

T. Sap in N.4.C. road junction and church Square in N.11.b. Hostile artillery active on houses T.3.C.4.3. Enemy working party on Sap N.9.C.5.4 fired on. Casualties inflicted as enemy were seen to take up dead or wounded.
Casualties - 1 O.R. wounded.

Saturday, 22nd Jan. 1916. at MAROC Sector RIGHT Subsector.

Quiet day. Officers patrol investigated supposed German listening post. 4 platoons LEINSTER attacked relieved by 4 other platoons same regt.
Casualties - Nil.

Sunday, 23rd Jan. 1916. at MAROC right subsector.

Quiet day. Hostile artillery active with L.H.V. + Shrapnell. Casualties. Lt. I.R. Bernard. (att'd 14.1.Bde. T.M.3.) wounded.

Monday, 24th Jan. 1916. at MAROC + BRACQUEMONT.

Occasional shelling of support line by enemy with heavy shrapnel and heavy H.E. 5"2 H.E.

failed to explode. Bn. relieved and moved into Bde. reserve at BRACQUEMENT (near NEUX LES MINES) Casualties - Nil.

Tuesday 25th Jan. 1916. at BRACQUEMENT.
Bn. in Bde. Reserve. Supplied working party of 3 Officers & 100 O.Rs. to work under R.E. at G.22.b. for whole day. 1 Officer and 26 ORs for R.E. Stn. LEVEL CROSSING, LES BREBES. 1 Officer and 30 O.Rs. for R.E. at Bully LES MINES Station. Casualties - Nil.

Wednesday 26th. Jan. 1916 at BRACQUEMENT.
Bn. in Bde. Reserve. Working Party of 3 Officers and 100 ORs. for work under R.E. on road from FOSSE 2 (K.29.a.8.4) to LES BREBES. Bn. at one hour's notice. G.O.C. 14th Bde. addresses all men whose period of service expires up to 31.3.16.
Casualties - Nil.

Thursday 27th Jan. 1916. BRACQUEMENT.
Bn. in Bde. Reserve. C.O. (Major H.E. Turner) reconnoitred LOOS sector prior to Bn. taking over on night 28/29-1-16. Casualties - Nil.

Friday 28th Jan. 1916. at BRACQUEMENT & LOOS.
Bn. in Bde. Reserve. Working party of 2 Officers and 100 men supplied for work under R.E. on road from FOSSE 2 to LES BREBIS. between 9am. and 12 noon. Arrived by 14th Bde. that Bn. in support in LOOS sects to to supply daily a Carrying party of one N.C.O. and 20 men for R.E. working on ST VINCENTS TUNNELS. Bn. moved from BRACQUEMENT at 4pm. and proceeded to relieve 2nd Bn. in support LOOS Sector. Two platoons of cyclists attached. Casualties - Nil.

Saturday
29th Jan. 1916. at LOOS.

Lt. F.W. Cripps took over command of "C" Coy.
Lt. W.A. Glaze took over command of Bombers.
Enemy reported to be cutting our wire at
M.3.a. 4.4. with field guns firing a round
every 10 seconds. 5th Div. report German
attempt to cut our wire at H.9.a. and that
enemy has cut diagonal lines in our wire.
Working Parties as under:-
3 officers and 100 OR for work under R.E.
1   "   2   "   "   "   18th Lon. Regt.
1   "   20 "   "   "   19th Lon. Regt.
1 Corp. for both with 19th Lon. Regt.
21 ORs for carrying party for R.E. working at
ST. VINCENTS TUNNELS.

Sunday
30th Jan. 1916. LOOS.

Hostile shelling intermittent during whole day.
Working Parties:- One Coy. at disposal of 15th Lon. Regt.
  "   "   "   "   "   "   19th "   "
  "   "   "   "   "   "   18th "   "
  "   "   "   "   "   "   2th   "   "

Casualties:- 3 ORs. wounded.

Monday.
31st Jan. 1916. at LOOS.

Quiet day. Stand-to fixed for 5 am and 4.30 pm.
Casualties – Nil.

Tuesday
1st. February 1916. at LOOS.

Dispositions same as on 31/1/16. Quiet day.
Slight shelling. Casualties – Nil.

Wednesday
2nd. February, 1916. at Loos.

Dispositions unchanged. Quiet day. Casualties – Nil.

Thursday
3rd. February 1916. at LOOS.

Dispositions unchanged. Salvo by bombards on
SNIPERS HOUSE between 2am & 3pm. Also on
enemy trenches South of the LENS Rd. 4 Platoons
MUNSTERS attached relieved by four platoons of
same regiment.

Casualties – 1 OR wounded.

Friday
Thursday 4th. February. 1916. LOOS.

Dispositions unchanged. Some artillery activity by enemy to which our artillery replied.
Casualties — Nil.

Saturday
Friday 5th. February. 1916. LOOS + LE BREBIS.

Dispositions unchanged. Quiet day. Bn. relieved by 7th. Lon. Regt. & moved into LES BREBIS.
Bn. in Bde. Reserve. Casualties — Nil.

Sunday
Saturday 6th. February 1916. LES BREBIS.

Bn. in Bde. Reserve at call of G.O.C. 140 Bde. Companies at disposal of Company Commanders.
Casualties — Nil.

Monday
Sunday 7th. February 1916. at LE BREBIS.

Bn. in Bde. Reserve. Parties totalling 5 Officers & 140 ORs. furnished for work under R.E. Village shelled slightly during day.
Casualties — Nil.

Tuesday
Monday 8th. Feb. at LES BREBIS.

Bn. in Bde. Reserve. Working Party of 2 Officers and 40 men supplied for work under R.E.
Casualties — Nil.

Wednesday
Tuesday 9th. Feb. 1916. LES BREBIS. + MAROC.

Bn. relieved 21st Lon. Regt. in MAROC Sector right sub sector — 4 platoons 9th. Royal DUBLIN FUS. attached — in support.
Casualties — Nil.

Thursday
Wednesday 10th. Feb. 1916. at MAROC.

Situation Quiet. Casualties, 1 OR. wounded.

Friday
Thursday 11th. Feb. 1916. at MAROC.

Quiet day. Salvo by the 18h. 1916 + 20h. Batteries followed by Salvo from one section each battery, followed by one round gunfire from 14th. Battery — all on road behind enemy's front line. Casualties — Nil.

Saturday 12th Feb. 1916. @ MAROC.
Quiet day – Our artillery replies to slight
shelling by L.H.V. Casualties – Nil.

Sunday 13th Feb. 1916. @ MAROC.
Quiet day. – Casualties – Nil.

Monday 14th Feb. 1916. @ MAROC.
Quiet day. Casualties – Nil.

Tuesday 15th Feb. 1916. @ MAROC & LESBREBIS.
Quiet day. Bn relieved by Loyal N. Lancs. Regt.
and moved into LESBREBIS.
Bn in Div. Reserve. Casualties – Nil.

Wednesday 16th Feb. 1916. @ LESBREBIS + BURBURE.
Bn moved into Army Reserve. Bn. moved
in billets @ BURBURE. Left LESBREBIS at about
1.15pm. to march to NOEUX-LES-MINES.
Entrained at NOEUX at 2.35pm.; detrained at
LILLERS and arrived at BURBURE at 4.15pm.
Casualties Nil.

Thursday 17th Feb. 1916 @ BURBURE.
In Army Reserve. Companies @ disposal of
Company Commanders, for cleaning and
refitting +c. Casualties – Nil.

Friday 18th Feb. 1916 @ BURBURE.
In Army Reserve. Drafts which had joined
Bn. during January and February inspected
by Commanding Officer. Companies @
disposal of Company Commanders.
Casualties – Nil.

Saturday 19th Feb. 1916. @ BURBURE.
In Army Reserve. Companies at disposal
of Company Commanders for training.
N.C.O.s class of instruction under Major
Turner. Casualties – Nil.

Sunday. 20th February 1916 @ BURBURE.

In Army Reserve. Divine Service of all denominations. Service for Jewish Soldiers by Senior Chaplain. (REV. M. ADLER).
@ LILLERS. — Casualties – Nil.

Monday. 21st. February. 1916. @ BURBURE.

In Army Reserve. Companies at disposal of Company Commanders for training. N.C.O's class under Major Turner. Casualties – Nil.

Tuesday. 22nd. February. @ BURBURE.

In Army Reserve. B⁰ Route March. Route:–
RAIMBERT. C:9:a:4:5: cross roads – FERFAY –
B.2.C.8.9 cross roads – POSSE 3 de FERFAY –
HURIONVILLE – BURBURE. N.C.O's class under Major Turner. Casualties – Nil.

Wednesday. 23rd February @ BURBURE.

In Army Reserve. Companies at disposal of Company Commanders for training. N.C.O's under Major Turner. Casualties – Nil.

Thursday. 24th. February. @ BURBURE.

In Army Reserve. 3 Officers and 120 O.R. supplies for work @ AUCHEL. Remainder of Bn. for training under Company Commanders. N.C.O's class under Major Turner. Casualties – Nil.

Friday. 25th. February. 1916. @ BURBURE.

In Army Reserve. 4 Officers and 150 O.R. for work @ HK⁹.SD¹ & M⁹R. flying Ground. Remainder of Bn. for training under Company Commanders. N.C.O's class under Major Turner.

Saturday 26th February 1916. @ BURBURE.

In Army Reserve. Working parts of 1 Officer and 50 O.R. for work @ R.E. yard MINX. Remainder of Bn. & training under Company Commanders. N.C.O's class under Major Turner. Casualties - Nil.

Sunday 27th February 1916. @ BURBURE.

In Army Reserve. Divine Service for all Denominations including Service for Jewish Soldiers at LILLERS. Casualties - Nil.

Monday 28th February 1916. @ BURBURE.

In Army Reserve. Companies at disposal of Company Commanders. N.C.O's under Major Turner. Casualties - Nil.

Tuesday 29th February 1916. @ BURBURE.

In Army Reserve. Bn. took part in Bde. Route March. Route - RAIMBERT- AUCHEL- MARLES- LES- MINES- LOZINGHEM- AUCHEL- RAIMBERT- BURBURE. Casualties - Nil.

Wednesday 1st March 1916. @ BURBURE.

Bn. in Army Reserve. Companies @ disposal of Company Commanders. Casualties - Nil.

Thursday 2nd March 1916 @ BURBURE.

Bn. in Army Reserve. Companies at disposal of Company Commanders. Casualties - Nil.

Friday 3rd March 1916. @ BURBURE.

Bn. in Army Reserve. Companies @ disposal of Company Commanders. Casualties - Nil. Conference of Bn. Comdrs. @ 4 pm @ 141 Bde Hq.

Saturday 4th March 1916 @ BURBURE + BOMY.

Bde. moved to 1st Army Training Area.
Bn. paraded @ 8.45 a.m. and marched
to billets at BOMY via - BURBURE - HURION - SHEET 5A HAZEBROUK
VILLE - BELLARY - AUCHY AU BOIS - RELY -
ESTREE BLANCHE - ENQUIN LES MINES - ERNY ST
JULIEN - BOMY. Casualties - Nil.

Sunday 5th March 1916. @ BOMY.

Bn. in 1st Army Training Area. Morning -
Tactical Exercises under Company Comdtt.
Afternoon. Bn. Tactical Exercises.
Casualties - Nil.

Monday 6th March 1916. @ BOMY.

Bn. in 1st Army Training Area. Morning -
Tactical Exercises under Coy. Comdts.
Afternoon. Bn. Tactical Exercises -
Close defence of village (BOMY)
Casualties - Nil.

Tuesday 7th March 1916 @ BOMY.

Bn. in 1st Army Training Area. Morning -
Tactical Exercises under Coy. Comdrs.
Afternoon. Bn. Tactical Exercises. Casualties
Nil.

Wednesday, 8th March 1916. @ BOMY.

Bn. in 1st Army Training Area. Bn. took
part in Bde. Tactical Exercise.
Casualties - Nil.

Thursday, 9th March 1916 @ BOMY & SAINS LES PERNES.

Bn. paraded @ 9.10 a.m. and moved to
billets @ SAINS LES PERNES for one night.
Casualties. Nil. with Bn. (4 killed + 3 wounded. Men
attached to 173rd R.E. Fld. Co.

Friday 10th March @ SAINS LES PERNES & CAMBLAIN CHATELAIN.

Bn. paraded at 11 a.m. and moved to billets @
CAMBLAIN CHATELAIN. Casualties - Nil.

Saturday 11th. March. 1916. @ CHAMBLAIN CHATELAIN.

Companies at disposal of Company Commandant.
Casualties – NIL.

Sunday. 12th. March. 1916. @ CHAMBLAIN CHATELAIN.
Divine Service @ CHAMBLAIN CHATELAIN.
Holy Communion @ LALONNE – RICQUART.
Casualties – NIL.

Monday. 13th March. @ CHAMBLAIN CHATELAIN.
Bn. bathed. Party sent to BRUAY to witness
distribution of decorations by G.O.C. 1st Army.
Sgt. Wood of "D" Coy. is awarded D.C.M.
Casualties – NIL.

Tuesday 14th. March 1916. @ CHAMBLAIN CHATELAIN
Companies at disposal of Company Commdrs.
Bn. Scouts reformed under 2nd Lt. W. L. DOUGLAS.
Casualties – NIL.

Wednesday. 15th March 1916. @ CHAMBLAIN CHATELAIN & VILLERS AU BOIS.
Division relieved 23rd. Divn. Bn. marched from CHAMBLAIN
at 7.30am. to relieve 12th SHERWOOD FORRESTERS – Route –
DIVION – HOUDAIN – PRESTICOURT – GRAND SERVINS –
VILLERS AU BOIS.

Thursday 16th March. 1916. @ VILLERS AU BOIS & CARENCY SECTOR
Bn. relieved 8th Bn. in left Subsector CARENCY SECTOR
disposition :– Front Line B Coy – QUARRIES – C Coy – SUPPORT (SUNKEN
RD) A Coy – Reserve (ABLAIN ST NAZAIRE) D Coy. Casualties – NIL.

Friday 17th March 1916. Dispositions Unchanged.
Enemy fired on Front Line from 11am to 12 noon
with Trench Mortars from 5pm to 6pm with H.V.
At night C Coy. relieved B Coy in Front Line & B.
Coy. moved into QUARRIES. Casualties – NIL.

Saturday 18th CARENCY SECTOR
Enemy shelled our trenches with aerial torpedoes,
trench mortars & H.V. At night D Coy.

March.

Relieved 'B' Coy. in Front line by 'B' Coy. relieved 'C' Coy. in QUARRIES. Casualties - 1 O.R. (att. to 141 M.G. Coy.) killed. 3 O.Rs. wounded.

Sunday 19th — CARENCY SECTOR

'A' Coy. relieved 'D' Coy. in Front Line. At night enemy sent up our S.O.S. Signal. Our Artillery immediately bombarded the enemy. Casualties 2 O.Rs. killed 2 O.Rs. wounded.

Monday 20th — CARENCY SECTOR & VILLERS AU BOIS.

Bn. relieved by 1st Bn. London Regt. and moved into billets at VILLERS AU BOIS for the night. (Over day). Casualties 2 O.Rs. wounded.

Tuesday 21st — VILLERS AU BOIS & FRESNICOURT.

Bde. in Div. reserve. Bn. moved to billets at FRESNICOURT via GRAND SERVINS. Casualties Nil.

Wednesday 22nd @ FRESNICOURT.

In Div. reserve. Coy. @ disposal of Coy. Comdrs. Casualties - Nil.

Thursday 23rd @ FRESNICOURT.

In Div. reserve. Working Party of 1 Offr. & 60 O.Rs. supplied to B.E.O. & party of 6 Offrs. & 350 O.Rs. supplied to 138th A.T.Coy. R.E. Casualties - Nil.

Friday 24th @ FRESNICOURT.

Bn. inspected by Comdg. Offr. Casualties - Nil.

Saturday 25th @ FRESNICOURT.

Bde. inspected by Corps. Comdt. @ OHAIN. Working Party of 2 Offrs. & 100 men supplied to 138th A.T.Coy. R.E. Casualties - Nil.

Sunday 26th @ FRESNICOURT.

Divine Service for All denominations. Casualties - Nil.

March.

Monday 24th. @ FRESNICOURT. & VILLERS AU BOIS.

Bde. relieved 1+2nd Bde. Bn. moved into
Support @ VILLERS AU BOIS. Casualties - Nil.

Tuesday 28th @ VILLERS A. B.—

In Support CARENCY SECTOR. Working party of
250. O.Rs. supplied to 2/3rd Lon. R.E. at CABARET
ROUGE. at 8.P.m. Casualties - Nil.

Wednesday 29th. @ VILLERS A B.

Working Parties totalling 250. O.Rs. supplied
for R.E. and Bde. HQ. Casualties- Nil.

Thursday 30th @ VILLERS A - B-

Working Party of 250. O.Rs. supplied to 2/3. R.E.
at CABARET ROUGE @ 8.P.m. Casualties- Nil.

Friday 31st @ VILLERS A. B.

Llamming ful demonstration @ QUOY SEEY MES

April

Attended by 1 Offr and about 80. O.Rs.
Casualties - Nil.

Saturday 1st April 1916 @ VILLERS AU BOIS & CARENCY SECTOR.

Bn. in Support. Bn. relieved at night by 1/5.Bn.
and proceeded to relieve 2nd London in C. subsector
CARENCY SECTOR, meeting guides of that Bn. at S.J.a. 8.2.
at 10 P.m. Casualties - Nil.

Sunday 2nd CARENCY SECTOR.

Bn. in Line. Artillery activity both sides at
night. Ration parties delayed by heavy enemy
shelling - Casualties - Nil.

Monday 3rd. CAR. SEC.

Bn. in Line. Nothing special to report. Casualties
2/Lt. Cib. Slight + 2 O.Rs. wounded.

Tuesday 4th CAR. SEC.

Quiet day - Nothing special to report - Casualties - Nil.

August

CARENCY SECTOR

Wednesday 5th

Bn. in line. Artillery "Strafe" organised by Bde. Carried out at intervals during the day on trenches & road junctions in enemy area. Continued at night on night targets arranged by artillery. Lt.Col. Strange S.O. - O.C. 9/5th Lond.Regt. visited Sect. Casualties Nil.

Thursday 6th

ditto. SEC?

Heavy shelling of QUARRIES intermittently by shrapnel intermittently during the day. Casualties 2 M.B. wounded

Friday 7th @ CARENCY SECTOR & VILLERS.

Bn. in line. Col. Strange left Bn. on termination of visit. At night L.t.B. relieved Bn. Guides sent to meet L.t.Bn. @ S.7. d.8.2 @ 10 p.m. Bn. marched to Support Billets at VILLERS A.D. B.013. Relief complete 2/30 am. Casualties wounded 2 O.R.s. 1 self inflicted.

Saturday 8th @ VILLERS & FRESNICOURT.

Bn. in Support. Bn. relieved in Support by 8.R. Bn. and marched to billets in Div. Reserve at FRESNICOURT 2 p.m. Permanent Working Party of 1 Offr & 65 O.R.s stayed behind in VILLERS for work under C.R.E. 47 (Lon.) R&B.Dr. Casualties - Nil.

Sunday 9th @ FRESNICOURT.

Coys. @ disposal of Coy. Comdrs. for cleaning up etc Working Parties of 5 Officers & 250 O.R.s supplied for work with 4th R.N.F. Casualties - Nil.

Monday 10th @ FRESNICOURT.

Working party of 2 Offrs & 200 O.R.s supplied to 185-11 T. Coy. R.E. Casualties Nil.

Tuesday 11th @ FRESNICOURT.

Coys @ disposal of Coy. Comdrs. Casualties Nil.

Wednesday 12th @ FRESNICOURT

Coys. practicing musketry. Working Party of 3 offrs. & 125 ORs. supplied to 135th A.T. Coy. R.E. Casualties - Nil.

Thursday 13th @ FRESNICOURT.

Working party of 3 offrs. & 200 ORs. supplied to 135th A.T. Coy. R.E. Party of 5 offrs. and 250 ORs supplied to 4th R.N.F. Casualties - Nil

Friday 14th. @ FRESNICOURT & VILLERS

In Div. Reserve. Working party of 1 offr & 1 N.C.O. & 30 men supplied to 2nd R.E. Dump Coy. SERVINS. Bn. moved into support and took over new Billets from 2/6 Bn. at VILLERS. at 6pm. Casualties - Nil.

Saturday 15th @ VILLERS.

Bn. in Support. Carrying party of 2 offrs. & 100 ORs. supplied to 146th Trenching Coy. R.E. casualties for Casualties - Nil.

Sunday 16th @ VILLERS.

Carrying party of 2 offrs & 100 ORs. supplied to 146 Tren. Coy. Casualties - Nil.

Monday 17th. @ VILLERS.

Carrying Party of 2 offrs + 100 ORs supplied to 146th Tren. Coy. Letter for all Offrs of Bde banned at 6h. for Field Ambulance. Casualties Nil.

Tuesday 18th NILLERS

Working Party of 100 ORs supplied to 135 AT Coy R.E.; C.O.s of all Bns. of Bde. interviewed by Brigadier at Bde. H.Q. Casualties - Nil.

Wednesday 19th @ VILLERS & CARENCY SECTOR

Bn. in Support. At night Bn. relieved 2/7 th in L. SubS, CARENCY Sector. Meeting guides of that Bn. @ Sugar Factory @ 9 pm. Casualties - 1 OR killed

CARENCY SECTOR

Thursday 20th @ CARENCY SECTOR
Bn. in Line. Permanent working Party 2 N.C.Os. & 30 O.Rs. supplied to 138.A.T. Coy. @ Gory SERVINS. Quiet day. Nothing Special to Report. Casualties - Nil.

Friday 21st @ CARENCY.
Organised staff of enemy's communications carried out by our artillery. An act. Bn. arrangements. Casualties Nil.

Saturday 22nd @ CARENCY.
Arc organised staffe of enemy's Communications Casualties - Nil.

Sunday 23rd @ CARENCY
Bombardment by Artillery of Enemy Support Line at S.2.6. @ 12.30am. @ night organised Staffe of enemy communications. Casualties 1 Ot Killed 1 Ot wounded

Monday 24th @ CARENCY.
At night organised shelling of enemy's communications. Casualties - Nil.

Tuesday 25th @ CARENCY & VILLERS.
At night Bn. relieved by 13th Bn. at 9pm. & moved into Support Billets @ VILLERS AU BOIS. Casualties - Nil.

Wednesday 26th @ VILLERS & FRESNICOURT.
Bn. relieved in support by 14.Bn. and marched to Auxy @ 2pm. to Billets in Div. Reserve @ FRESNICOURT. Permanent working Party of 1 Offr. + 65 ORs. detailed for work under CRE On 3/4/16 relieved by party of same strength. Casualties - Nil.

Thursday 27th @ FRESNICOURT
Bn. in Div. Reserve. Working Party of 4 Offrs. & 250 ORs supplied to 23rd RE. party of 4 Offrs. & 200 ORs supplied to 4th RSF. Casualties Nil.

April

Friday 28th @ FRESNICOURT.

Inspection by C.O. in preparation for inspection by G.O.C. 47th Div. Casualties - Nil.

Saturday 29th. @ FRESNICOURT.

Inspection of Bn. by G.O.C. 47th Div. @ OLHAIN followed by march past. Inspection of Bn. in Fire Yet. by C.O.C. 47th Div. @ OLHAIN. Working party 6 Offrs. + 300 O.Rs. supplies 6 with Res. 4. Casualties - Nil.

Sunday 30th @ FRESNICOURT.

Divine Service for all denominations. Casualties Nil.

Monday 1st May 1916 @ FRESNICOURT.

Bn. in Div. Reserve. Bn. firing on Range. Working Party of 4 Offrs + 200 O.Rs. supplied to R.Es. Similar party supplies to R.W.F. Casualties - Nil.

Tuesday 2nd @ FRESNICOURT & VILLERS.

Bn. moved into Support @ VILLERS AU BOIS. At night every available man on working party. carrying up material under R.E. preparatory to blowing up of 3 mines. Casualties - Nil.

Wednesday 3rd @ VILLERS.

Bn. stood to @ 4/30 P.M. mines referred to above were successfully exploded at 5 P.M. Casualties - Nil.

Tuesday 4th. @ VILLERS.

Working Party of 1 Sgt. + 25 O.Rs. supplies to C.R.E. Casualties. Nil.

MAY

Friday 5th. @ VILLERS.
Quiet day. Casualties - Nil.

Saturday 6th. @ VILLERS.
Working party of 1 Offr & 25 OR supplied
to Tunneling Coy R.E. Casualties - Nil.

Sunday 7th. @ VILLERS. & CARENCY SECTOR.
C of E Services in morning. At night Bn.
relieved 23rd. London Regt in CARENCY SECTOR,
left Subsector, with 1 Coy in Front Line
1 Coy in QUARRIES. 2 Coys in ABLAIN.
Casualties - Nil.

Monday 8th. @ CARENCY
Very Quiet day. Slight minenwerfer activity.
Casualties - Nil.

Tuesday 9th. @ CARENCY
Disposition unchanged. Situation Quiet and
normal. Casualties 10R killed 6 OR wounded

Wednesday 10th @ VILLERS CARENCY
Disposition unchanged. Situation Quiet.
Casualties. 1 OR wounded.

Thursday 11th. @ CARENCY
Situation Quiet & Normal. Casualties Nil

Friday 12th @ CARENCY
Situation Quiet & Normal. Casualties - 1 OR Killed

Saturday 13th. @ CARENCY & VILLERS.
Situation Quiet & Normal. Bn. relieved by 22nd Bn
& moved into billets @ VILLERS. Casualties 4 OR wounded

Sunday 14th. @ VILLERS & VERDREL.
Bn. moved into Bde Reserve at VERDREL.
Casualties 1th

MAY

Monday 15th @ VERDREL.

Bn. in Div. Reserve. Bkds @ FRESNICOURT. available for Bn. training of Reserve Sections for Lewis Guns & Bombers commenced. Medical Inspection of whole Bn. 3 Offrs & 200 ORs supplied for working party to R.E. Casualties - Nil.

Tuesday 16th @ VERDREL.

Training of Reserves for Specialist Sections continued. One Offr & 10 men attended presentation of Medal Ribbons by Army Comdr. at Bruay. C.O. & 2 Senior Captains attended interviews by Brigadier @ Bde. H.Q. on subject of Court Martial. A.D.V.S. lectured men of Transport Section @ Bt. Lon. L. H. Casualties Nil.

Wednesday 17th @ VERDREL.

Coys. @ disposal of Coy Comdrs. G.O.C. 14. Bde. inspected animals of each Bn. Transport (Stripped) on 17th Line.

Right working party of 3 Offrs & 200 ORs supplied to R.E's. Casualties Nil.

Thursday 18th @ VERDREL.

Bn. (less men on working party 17th inst) and men on Lewis demonstration) fired on range under Capt Chandler. Lewis demonstration by 2/Lt. Eitzen in accordance with scheme received from Bde. Lecture by Capt Croft to all Officers & N.C.O's. on "Trench Discipline." O.C. Bn. interviewed by Brigadier. Corps Comdr. not yet approved of work done in connection with mining operations of 3rd inst. received and communicated to all ranks. Casualties Nil.

Friday 19th @ VERDREL & FOSY SERVINS.

Bn. moved into Support. Took over billets from Sk. Bn. Whole day working. Party of 5 O.T.O. supplied to R.E. Capt Boulter (2d in command) lectured all officers who joined Bn. subsequent to Bn. arriving in France. Officers reconnoitred

CARENCY-Bnds Subsector. Casualties 1916.

Saturday 20th. @ Gouy Servins-VILLERS + CARENCY.

Bn moved at about 10 P.m. to VILLERS and at night relieved 2nd Can Regt. in CARENCY. Centre Subsector. Casualties 5 ORs wounded.

Sunday 21st @ CARENCY May 1916

Right + Reserve Coys. heavily shelled + nine-Coys-fired. Artillery + medium T.M.S. retaliate. Shelling r. of Right Reserve Coy. Continued until 9/30 P.m. Front Support + Reserve Lines all very heavily shelled by enemy with all types of Artillery nearly all day. Enemy attacked Right Bn. and succeed in pushing line in Centre thigh of Subsector & gain a footing in craters Front Support Line. Casualties. 5 ORs wounded

Monday 22nd @ CARENCY.

Between 1/30 AM. + 2/30 AM. Right Bn Counter attacked + regained their line except for a small portion of Front Support Line on right of Subsector. During these operations Bn. on Right were heavily attacked & forced to retire from Front, Support + a portion of Reserve Lines. Counter attack failed. Subsection occupied by this Bn. was heavily shelled throughout but no attack was developed. Front Line of Right Coy. was badly damaged and communication trenches VEN CUT + VIVIER. also flattened in places. Lachrymatory Shells were used in large numbers by enemy. The Valley was full of gas until 5 P.m. All preparations for meeting a Gas attack were made, but apparently nothing was used in attack. About 2/30 AM. Situation was again fairly quiet, enemy artillery was active throughout the day, activity being replied to by enemy. Casualties. Capt Boyd, wounded - stay remained at duty. 5 ORs killed 32 ORs wounded.

MAY

Tuesday 23rd @ CARENCY

Enemy artillery fairly active. Our artillery firing throughout day on lines captured by enemy. At 8.25 p.m. troops on right counter attacked to regain lost line - attack failed. Heavy firing continued intermittently until midnight. Snipers reported our enemy crawl work on his mine gallery about Sap 136 from 9 p.m. until about 5 a.m. when work was resumed. Casualties 4 OR wounded.

Wednesday 24th @ CARENCY

Situation more quiet. Enemy artillery + m. guns active. (Fired of the Bn. recommenced line normal. Casualties 6 OR wounded

Thursday 25th @ CARENCY

Situation normal. Minenwerfer activity about noon. Artillery reported activity behind MOMBA CRATER - probably enemy working party. At night Bn. Snipers

Relieved by 13h. Essex and moved to billets @ MAISNEL BOUCHE, arriving about 3 a.m. 26/5/16. Casualties 4 OR wounded.

Friday 26th @ MAISNEL BOUCHE + DIEVAL.

At 2.30 p.m. Bn. left MAISNEL and marched to billets at DIEVAL in corps Reserve - arriving about 10 p.m. Casualties - Nil.

Saturday 27th @ DIEVAL.

Bn. in corps Reserve. Coy @ disposal of Coy Comdr. for cleaning up repairing. Casualties - Nil.

Sunday 28th @ DIEVAL.

Divine Service. Casualties Nil.

Monday 29th @ DIEVAL.

Coys @ disposal of Coy Comdrs. for cleaning up refitting + inspections etc. One Heavy withdrawn from each man & Lt Col Norman took over

1917

Temporary Command of 14th Bn. & hospl
I.C. Ranan Temp. Comd. of Bn. vice
Capt. P.C. Bowes on second in command.
Casualties Nil.

Tuesday 30th @ Dr E VAL

Bn. out all day training. Inoculation
of men who had not been inoculated during
previous 12 months. proceeded with.
Casualties Nil.

Wednesday 31st @ Dr E VAL

Bn. continue training under Coy
Comdrs. Casualties - Nil.

Thursday 1st JUNE @ Dr E VAL.

Whole Bn. Bathed at Chateau LA COMPTE.
Casualties Nil.

Friday 2nd. @ Dr E VAL.

Bn. Training under Coy Comdr. Specialists
Comars. Casualties Nil.

Saturday 3rd. @ Dr E VAL

Bn. Training under Coy. Coy Comr. Specialist
Comars. Casualties - Nil.

Sunday 4th. @ Dr E VAL.

Divine Services. 2 Offrs + 20 ORs proceed
to PERNES for attachment to 2nd Inown Regt.

Monday 5th. @ Dr E VAL

Bn. training under Coy Comars + Specialist
Comars. Capt Brough placed in charge of Res.

JUNE.

Class of field engineering - class attended by ~ Offrs + N.C.Os per Bn. Commanded by Lt. Col. Norman assumed command of Bn. Casualties - Nil.

Tuesday 6th. @ DIEVAL

All work some arrears owing to wet weather. Casualties Nil.

Wednesday 7th. @ DIEVAL

Bn. attended Bde. ceremonial parade. Medal Ribbons presented to N.C.Os & men who have received decorations - presentation by G.O.C. 141 Bde. Information received from Bde. Intd. of death of Lce Nishimura. Casualties Nil.

Thursday 8th. @ DIEVAL.

Bn. bathed @ CORTON. Casualties Nil.

Friday 9th. @ DIEVAL.

Training carried out usual by Coys + Specialist sections. Casualties Nil.

Saturday 10th. @ DIEVAL

C.O. visited line to be taken over by Bn. Coys + Sections @ disposal of respective Comdrs for detailed inspection to ensure that each man is fully equipped. Casualties Nil.

Sunday 11th. @ DIEVAL + FOSSE 10

Bn. left DIEVAL @ 8am to FOSSE 10. 1 Sgt + 2 Ors. took over light railway station @ B.U.+T from 2/4 Bn. Bde. Casualties Nil.

Monday 12th @ FOSSE 10 + BULLY

Bde. took over ANGRES section from 24th Bde. Bn. moved into support role in BULLY - 2 Coys in CORON D'AIX; 1 Coy in MECHANICS + 1 Coy in GAPA PONT. relieving 1st SHERWOOD FORESTERS. Casualties Nil.

Tuesday 13th @ BULLY.

Bn. in Support. Enemy Quiet. Our T.M's
+ Artillery @ 9 pm bombarded enemy support
line between M.20.b.3.0. & M.20.b.3.3.
Working Party of 2 Offrs & 100 men furnished
to work on cleaning of BATTLE LINE.
Casualties Nil.

Wednesday 14th @ BULLY.

Working party as on 13th to work on
BATTLE LINE. Permanent working party
of 1 Offr & 25 ORs supplied to R.E.
Armies in France adopted time ordered by
Algrs of French Government, + at 11 P.M. time
was advanced one hour, making 11 PM
midnight. Casualties Nil.

Thursday 15th @ BULLY.

Situation Quiet. P.W.P. supplied as
1st. Unit of 1 Offr. & 25 ORs withdrawn
+ replaced by 1 Offr. & 3 S.O.R. supplied

to H.L R.E. night working party of 4 Offrs
+ 200 OR. supplied to R.E. Casualties Nil.

Friday 16th. @ BULLY.

Situation Quiet. Casualties. Nil.

Saturday 17th. @ BULLY + FOSSE 10

Bn. relieved by 21st. Bn. And moved
into reserve billets at FOSSE 10. Coys
marching by sections @ 100 yds interval.
Working party of 1 Off. & 3 S.O.R. supplied
to H.L.R.E. & night working party of
4 Offrs & 200 OR. supplied to R.E.
Casualties — NIL.

Sunday 18th. @ FOSSE 10.

Divine Service in Church Army Hut.
Medical Inspection of Men
of Bn. Casualties Nil.

JUNE.

Monday 19th. @ FOSSE 10.
Bn. @ disposal of Bgr Comdr.
At 3/30.P.m. Major General decorated
Officers & men awarded decoration.
1 Off. 10 min attended, in addition
to following who received decoration
(ribbon)

Capt. Crofts.   MILITARY CROSS.

2357. Pte J. Read.   MILITARY MEDAL
2360. "   J. Lloyd.   do
2355. "   L. Millett   do
4761. "   W.T. Wolfort   do
2008. "   J. Beasley.   do
3482. "   A. Poste.   do

Night working parties of 2 Offrs & 100 O.R.
supplied to carry up 1m.T.M.B. & 5 Offrs
& 250 O.R. for R.E. Casualties Nil.

Tuesday 20th. @ FOSSE 10.
Recovn. boys at disposal
Bn. in Reserve. boys. Bombers under Bn.
boy bomber. Off. practised hurling of Live
bombing. Off. practised hurling of Live
bombs at Bde. Bomb. Sch. Working
of 50 men at 4pm to R.E. and 4 Offrs. and
248 O.R. to R.E. at night. Casualties Nil.

Wednesday 21st. FOSSE 10.
Bn. relieved 24th Lon Regt. in Left Subsector
AYGRES S SecR51 with HQs in BULLY ALLEY, 3
Coys. in front line, & Support Coy. in MOROCCO
SOUTH. Slight minenwerfer & Rifle Grenade
activity during day to which our artly.
relied. Casualties 1/4 wounded.

Thursday 22nd JUNE. AYGRES 2. Subsec51.
Considerable activity by enemy with
Minenwerfer, T.M. & Rifle Grenades. Eleven
aeroplanes flying very high passed over
our line at 1.45 P.M. 4 NCOs. & 24 men
supplied to R.E. as dug-out squad- This
party reported to R.E. for same work each
day until end of this tour of duty.
Casualties 5 O.R. wounded.

Friday 23rd June. AYGRES. L Subsec51.
Intermittent enemy activity with minenwerfers
Rifle Grenades. Party of one officer & 36 O.R.
and party of one officer & 44 O.R. sent to
186. Gas School for instruction in
lighting of Smoke Candles & Bombs.
50. O.R. supplied to carry up Smoke
Candles. Party of bomber of 40 men.

26th June 1916. In Bde Reserve.
Two minutes bombardment of enemy front & rear communication trenches along our front. Coy at disposal of Bn. Comdr.
Casualties - OR killed 1.

27th June 1916. In Bde Reserve.
After bombardment of enemy lines & discharge of Gas & smoke, raiding party supplied from Bn. of Rifle raided enemy frontline opposite Bde Front. Party successfully entered enemy trenches, and after bombing dugouts etc returned to our line with slight casualties. Raid successful. Casualties - OR wounded 1.

28th June/July 1916. In Bde Reserve.
300 men of 170 Bde. employed to remove Gas cylinders from line at 9/30 a.m. our heavies bombarded enemy billets, from 10/15 AM to 12/30 AM. Artillery fired Salvos at about 20 minute intervals on selected points. Working party of 1 Off. + 30 OR. supplied at 10/30 PM to

supplied to Tun. Coy. Casualties - 1 OR. Killed.

SATURDAY 24th JUNE. AtGRES L Subsects.
Considerable Rifle Grenade activity by enemy from 10/30 A.M. to 12 noon. At 11 A.M.
RE: Blew up a # camouflet to destroy enemy gallery. Operation apparently successful as sounds of digging were heard - presumably enemy digging to get out their men. Our Arty: bombarded German front line at 11 P.M.
16 OR. supplied for carrying up Smoke candles - Casualties Casualties Nil.

SUNDAY 25th JUNE. AtGRES. L Subsects.
Bn. relieved by 19R. Bn. & moved into Reserve, with HQ. at SAINS BOUVIGNY. 2 Coys. at BULLY 1 Coy at CARON D'AS & one Coy home at section Bombers in front line at disposal of 19R.Batn. 16 OR. supplied to carry up Smoke Candles as on 23 inst. Parties who proceeded to Div. Gas Sch. on 23rd inst.

War Diary.

From 1st August 1916
To 18-10-16

Officer i/c wagons at Mechanics Dump.
Casualties: Offr. wounded - O.R. 10 wounded
(includes 21 Latham & 4 Offr. Signal attd.
14101 + T.W.B.)

27th June 1916.   Support.
Bn. relieved 18th Don. in Support with
HQ at Bully. 1½ Coys at Braun Stak
½ Coy at G.H.Q. dugout. 1 Coy at
disposal of 20th Don in front Line.
Continued bombardments by our Heavy
Artillery during day, of enemy front.
Our Corps Artillery bombarded enemy
Artillery during night. Night working
party of 2 Offrs & 80 O.R. worked on
joining up Sap heads. Casualties Nil.

28th June 1916.   Support.
Party as 27th inst. for joining up Sap
heads. 2 E.O. & 8 L. Gunners: B.O.
& 2 sections of Bombers attd to Acheson Bn
in line. Support party of 1 Offr & 20 O.R.
supplied to VKo Casualties Nil.

1st August 1916   Monchaux & Bonnières
Bn. left Monchaux for Bonnières, passing
Bde Starting Point at St. Ouen at 7:30 a.m.
& Hayes at 9/30 AM. arriving in new
billets about 4:30 p.m. Casualties. Nil.

2nd August 1916.   Bonnières
Training under Coy Comdr. Casualties Nil.

3rd August 1916   Bonnières
Training under Coy Cmdrs. Casualties Nil.

4th August 1916.   Maison Ponthieu
Bn. left Bonnières at 5 AM for Maison
Ponthieu, passing Bde Starting point at
Villers L'Hôpital at 5/45 AM and arriving
in billets at about 11 AM. Casualties Nil.

5th August 1916   Maison Ponthieu & Hogenvillers
Bn. left Maison Ponthieu at 6/30 a.m. arriving
in new billets at Hogenvillers at about noon.
Casualties. Nil.

6th August 1916. Argenvillers
Training under Coy Comdrs. Divine Service
for C of E & Nonconformists. Casualties Nil.

7th August 1916. Argenvillers
Coy. Training including training in
Trench to Trench Attack. Casualties - Nil.

8th August 1916. Argenvillers
Coy Training including training in
Trench to Trench Attack. Casualties - Nil.

9th August 1916. Argenvillers
Bn. Training in Wood & Village fighting.
Casualties Nil.

10th August 1916. Argenvillers
Training by half Bn in Trench Attack.
Casualties Nil.

11th August 1916. Argenvillers
Bn. Training in Trench Attack.
Casualties Nil.

12th August 1916. Argenvillers
Bn. Training in morning. At 12 noon Bn.
paraded to take part in Fete. Scheme (Trench
Attack) Casualties - Nil. 2nd Lt Bailey joined Bn.

13th August 1916. Argenvillers
Training under Coy Comdrs. Casualties Nil.

14th August 1916. Argenvillers
Bn. Training. Tactical Scheme, including
Wood & Village fighting. Casualties - Nil.

15th August 1916. Argenvillers
Bn. Training. Casualties Nil.

16th August 1916. Argenvillers
Bn. Training. Casualties Nil.

17th August 1916. Argenvillers
Bn. Training. Route March. Casualties Nil.

18th August 1916. Argenvillers
Bn. Training. Capt F.K. Grimwood joined Bn. Casualties Nil.

10th August 1916. Hamelles
Bn. Training. Orders received for move on
20th. Casualties Nil.

21st August 1916. Bruchamp
Bn. paraded at 1/15 AM to move to
new billets at Bruchamp. Bn. was B
took part in Bde Scheme (Rear Guard
Exercise) returning in column of route
at 3rd August marching to Bruchamp.

21st August 1916. Monton Villers
Bn. paraded at 1/30 AM moved to new
billets at Monton Villers. Casualties Nil.

22nd August 1916. Purregot
Bn. paraded at 9am to move to Purregot
arriving at about 11 am. Casualties Nil.

23rd August 1916. Beale
Bn. paraded at 6/30 AM. and marched to
new billets at Beale. Casualties Nil.

24th August 1916. Beale
Bn. Training. Casualties Nil.

25th August 1916. Beale
Bn. Training. Casualties Nil.

26th August 1916. Beale
Bn. Training. Casualties Nil.
60 visited 3rd Corps Line.

27th August 1916. Beale
Bn. Training. Casualties Nil. Major Fowler
visited 3rd Corps Line.

28th August 1916. Beale
Bn. Training. Casualties Nil.

29th August 1916. Beale
Bn. Training. Casualties Nil.

30th August 1916. Beale
Bn. Training. Coy Cmdrs & Scout Officer
visited 3rd Corps Line. Casualties Nil.

31st August 1916. Breele
Bn. took part in Bde Practice Attack.
Casualties Nil.

1st September 1916. Breele
Bn. carried out Practice attack on frontage
of 300 yds. Transport inspected on
Transport Lines by G.O.C. 141st Bde.
Casualties Nil.

2nd September 1916. Breele
Bn. Training. Route March fatiguing.
Line Offrs. proceeded on tour of inspection
of forward area. Bn. Boxing Competition
commenced. Casualties Nil.

3rd September 1916. Breele
Divine Service for all Denominations
including Service by Senior Jewish
Chaplain for Jewish Soldiers. Bn.
Boxing Tournament Competition (finals)
completed. Casualties Nil.

4th September 1916. Breele
Coy. carried out Tactical Schemes during
morning. Bde Boxing tournament in
afternoon. Final of L. Weight Competition
won by Cpl. J. Murray of this Bn.
Bn. Tactical Scheme from 8PM to 10 PM.
Party of 1 NCO & 30 men supplied for
coy work under Town Mayor Casualties Nil.

5th September 1916. Breele
Bn. practiced Wood fighting & Musketry
instruction for backward men. Casualties Nil.

6th September 1916. Breele
Bn. took part in Div. Scheme Various
Scheme. 3 Offrs proceeded to reconnoitre
forward area (field. service dress) also
of 1 NCO & 12 men supplied to/for
London Rifles. Casualties Nil.

7th September 1916. Breele
Training under Coy Comdrs & C.C. Specialists
of Simmons proceeded to reconnoitre

Forward area. Working party of 1 Offr
& 110 O.R. supplied for work at Bazentin.
Party of 1 N.C.O. & 50 men supplied for
work under own Major. Casualties Nil.

9th September 1916. Boods
Br. took part in Bde Scheme. Br. Tactical
Scheme carried out at night. Casualties Nil.

10th September 1916. Boods
Br. took part in Bn. Bde- Major General
Subsequently service appreciation of work
done. Party of 1 N.C.O. & 50 men supplied
for work under own Major. Casualties Nil.

10th September 1916. Beals
Divine Service for all Denominations.
Five Offrs attended demonstration by
"Tanks". Casualties Nil.

11th September 1916. Support
Bn. relieved 3rd Bde in Support Area

Bn taking over billets in Mametz Wood
and at line transport at Becourt.
Five Offrs attended demonstration by
"Tanks". Casualties Nil.

12th September 1916. Mametz Wood
Station quiet. Carrying party supplied
for carrying up to line. O.R. killed 1.
Wounded 2.

13th September 1916. Mametz Wood
Quiet day. Br. Offr & pt Br. proceeded
with Major Wood (10th London) to recoinn
front line + men attacked as grave
diggers. Following carrying parties
attached for duty:-
    43 OR to R.O. at Bde Dump
    13   "   " 1st W.G.Cy.
    13   "   " 1st F.N.L.G.

Casualties - OR wounded 1
Capt. P.W. Downes took charge of work
of clearing the Battlefield.

14th September 1916. High Wood.

100th & 4th K. Inf. Bdes. relieved Hood Bde. in High Wood. Scots. Irish Bde took over from S.14.c.6.4 (Sap. exclusive) to S.13.d.2.9. 14th Bn. took over right sub-sector from S.14.c.6.4 to S.14.c.3.6 with 2 Coys. in front line & 2 Coys. in support of Cough Street running S.E. from junction of Chalk Street with Kendall Avenue. There a reserve Coy. move at 12 midnight to be in position at

Going on steadily since 12th inst.) became visible, & the Bn. launched an attack in 4 waves of 1 Coy. on a platoon frontage, with object of taking 1st & 2nd lines of trenches & constructing a strong point for 1 Platoon & 2 Vickers Guns at 14.34.d.1.1. Enemy met attack with very heavy M.G. fire. 4th attack was held up for nearly 2 hours till a fresh assault was made & all Bn. objectives reached about 10/30am.

Casualties Officers: 2/Lt. Killed
2/Lt. H. J. Hacket   2/Lt. Stirling
" F.C. Coates   " A. J. Hopwood
Wounded 2/Lt. Moore.   2/Lt. H. Hadden
2/Lt. J. H. S. Edwards " A. Courtauche
2. G. A. K. Smith.   Capt. Yarcroft.
O.R. Killed 65 Wounded 254.
Captures of Materiel included 3 field guns & 3 M.G.

15th September 1916.

1am. ready to be in position for attack on enemy's system on 15th inst. 47th Div. with New Zealand Div. on right & 50th Div. on left attacked enemy Defence System between Combles & Martinpuich, with the object of swinging Marval, Les Boeufs, Gueodecourt & Cdo. & breaking through the bottle system of defence. At 6/20 am. our artillery bombardment (which had been

16th September 1916.   High Wood.
Enemy shelled during morning very heavily. Transport moved up to Bottom Wood. Casualties Nil. Capt Crofts died of wounds.

14th September 1916.   Mametz Wood & Sur Bh Line
Bn relieved and marched back into Mametz Wood, arriving about 9 am. Bn left Mametz Wood at 4/20 AM to relieve 22nd Bn. at S4.c.25. Casualties Nil

15th September 1916. Sur 18h Line
Quiet day. Casualties Nil.

19th September 1916.   Sur 18h Line
Fairly quiet day until relief of Bn was commenced at night, when relief was considerably delayed by enemy shelling. Bn relieved at night by portions of 1st Bde 1st Cameron Relieps Coy of this Bn in front line & 10th

Clarkes & relieved, remaining 3 Coys Coy Kailed & Main Road at 52. Corner of Horton Wood, where not far was enemy line proceeded to billets at Albert arriving early in morning of 20th inst. Casualties Nil Wounded 1.

20th September 1916. Albert
Quiet day. Casualties Nil

21st September 1916.   Brele.
Bn proceeded to Brele taking over billets previously occupied there. Draft of 124 OR joined Bn. Carrying parties sent to 1st NLR & F.M.P. Bn met by Service Unit. Casualties Nil.

22nd September 1916.   Brele.
Day spent in clearing up & re-equipping. Draft (1 Offr Ward and 9 OR) joined Bn. Notices received that following had been awarded Military

Medal:-
2247 Sgt Amoaks G. Supg Sgt Palk. S.
1640 Rfn Smallman E 2233 Sgt Ballard R.
1034 CSM. Duguid D. 2233 Sgt Ballard R.
1069 Sgt Farnham J. 2918. Barron A.
2233 Rfn Berry B. 169. Rfn Cox. J.
Casualties Nil.

23rd September 1916.   Poole
New draft inspected by O.C. Hot. Bde.
2/7 Co. NCO men supplied fat works under
Van. Major. Casualties Nil.

24th September 1916.   Poole
Divine Service for all Denominations.
Coys & Specialist Sections cleaning
under Coy.Cr. Coy. inspected by
CO. at 3 pm. Casualties Nil.

25th September 1916.   Poole
Bn. took part in Bde. Ceremonial from
9/30 am. to 10/30 am. Remainder of day

spent in training to unrear Coy Comdr.
Lt P.K. Hards joined unit.

26th September 1916. Poole
Training under Coy Comdr. Draft (21
L/C Barnard & 2/7 Bn) joined unit
following preceded to Base H.Q. for
decoration with Military Medal by O/C
Hot Bde.
2334. Duguid (D)   Sgt Bard E.
Sgt Bango A.   Rfn Perry B.
Rfn Cox J.
Remainder of NCO men awarded
M.M. Could not attend for following reasons:
Sgt Amoates C.   Sgt Paks S.
Farnham E. to England.
Rfn Smallman E. 2918 L/C Barron.
Sgt Ballard R. Killed in action
15/9/16.   Casualties. Nil.

24th. September 1916. Trenches Hamely.
Form. Offrs. reconnoitred front line. Brigadier
held conference with Bn. Comdrs. at 9/30 am
Bn. moved up into Support, taking up
billets in Hamely Wood. Transport at
Bottom Wood. Casualties Nil.

25th. September 1916. Hamely
Bn. relieved 2nd. Royal Sussex Regt.
in line - Eaucourt L'Abbe. Casualties
1 O.R. Killed 2 O.R. wounded

26th. September 1916. Trenches before Eaucourt L'Abbe.
Fairly quiet day. Slight shelling of front
& support lines by enemy. Casualties Nil.

27th. September 1916. Trenches before E.L.
Situation normal. Enemy shelled with
5.9 howitzers. Casualties 20R Killed
18 wounded.

1st. October 1916. Trenches before Eaucourt L'Abbe.
Bn. in trenches. Fine weather. Skinful trench-
Front line immediately in front of Eaucourt L'Abbe.
Between 4/30 am Sept 30th & 4/30 am 1st Oct.
orders were issued in duplicate to each
Coy preparatory to the attack on Eaucourt
L'Abbe. At 5/15 am Bn. H.Q. moved
forward to Starfish trench. Separation of
Bn. immediately prior to the attack -
Front Line H.Q. - D.B. Coys. H.Q.s Coys.
each had 2 L. Guns & one section
Bombing Platoon. C & D Coys. each had
one Lewis Gun. In reserve at Porth St.
were 2 Lewis Guns & 2 Section's Bombers
as carrying party of 20 men.
2/Lt Constans with necessary numbers
forwarded to H.Q. of 9th Bn. for
Liaison Duties, but at here left bare
and formed a Look Out - telephone
station in Fine trench on midway between
Bn. H.Q. & front line to assist in the
maintenance of communication on the
event of forward telephone communication

2nd October 1916.   In Line

About mid-day Bn. was relieved by 8th. Bn. & returned to Starfish Line.

3rd October 1916.   In Line.

On night of 3rd Bn. reorganised into 2 Composite Coys, moved up prepared to take over but could not occupy their Support Line until afternoon of 4th owing to have got more than half way across No Mans Land when they were met by Snipers M.G. Fire. Small parties entered the German Front Line but were driven out by strong enemy bombing attacks. Eventually all had to withdraw to O.B.L.

4th October 1916.

The enemy placed a very heavy barrage on this line. When the barrage lifted the Stars Support line was occupied by H.Q. and posts, touch being obtained with 13th on the right, route 30 on the left. To right of 4th. Bn. was relieved by 15th. Bn. Hot tea was prepared ready for Bn. at Bazentin. Reliefs were completed in Starfish

---

as it was very shortly after Zero. No one at 5/15 A.m. knew that hour until 5 A.m. no reliable information was received from the front. At about 5 A.m. a report was received that the attack was held up by enemy bombing. All Coys went over punctually at Zero but no Coy. Officer to have got more than half way across No Mans Land when they were met by Snipers M.G. Fire. Small parties entered the German Front Line but were driven out by strong enemy bombing attacks. Eventually all had to withdraw to O.B.L.

Officer Casualties   Killed

2/Lt. C.A. Smith   2/Lt. R.L. Barnard 2/Lt. A.H. Thompson.

Wounded

2/Lt. A.M. Gutteridge.   2/Lt. N.J. Edwards.
2/Lt. G. Bailey   2/Lt. A.M. Laird, left Bn. with Shell Shock- but were subsequently reported as sick.

Wood on morning of Assist in work of clearing Ballyhow

5th October 1916
Total casualties from 1st to 4th Oct
Offr. killed 3 wounded 4 (see Oct 1st)
O.R. killed - 23 wounded 157 missing
100 wounded missing 1. OR load
146. Of the men reported missing are
since missing 4(11/16). casualties see
5th Nk.

6th October 1916   Hamel Wood
Bn in Hamel Wood. casualties Nk.
Working Parties supplied to RE.

7th October 1916   Mill Street
Bn moved at 9p.m. to Mill St with
500 Sh.to.s) atd casualties Nk

8th October 1916   Mill Street
Working Parties totalling 700 O.R. supplied.
Casualties O.R. wounded 2.
1 Offr + 10 O.R. supplied to HQ Bde 6

9th October 1916   Mill St
Working Parties totalling 700 O.R. supplied
Casualties Nk.

10th October 1916   Mill St
Working Parties totalling 700 O.R. supplied
Casualties O.R. killed 4 wounded 7
missing 3. The four men killed +
7 wounded were caused by premature
explosion of shell fired by S.A.A.
at 8.30 & 20.40 received conveying Major
Generals hearty appreciation from Bde.
by Division during past 10 days -
especially emphasizing the capture of
Gair Court + cottages.

11th October 1916   Franvillers
Bn moved from Mill St into Reserve
billets at Franvillers.
Casualties Nk.

1st July 1916. Morlancourt + Bonnets

2nd October 1916. Hamel-Les
Coy. inspected during the morning by
C.O. Bn. inspected (in clean fatigue)
by Corps Comd. Casualties Nil.

13th October 1916. Hamel-Les
Coys. at disposal of Coy Comdrs.
Transport moved off to ST SAUVEUR en
route to new billeting area. Casualties Nil.

14th October 1916. Franvillers
Bn. marched from Franvillers at 11am
at entrained at Albert for reinstalling
area. Casualties Nil.

15th October 1916. Bresne Bresne
Bn. detrained at Longpré and marched
to billets at Bresne Bresne arriving
in the evening. Casualties Nil.

16th October 1916. Bresne Bresne
Bn. resting. Casualties Nil.

www.ingramcontent.com/pod-product-compliance
Lightning Source LLC
Chambersburg PA
CBHW081546160426
43191CB00011B/1850